PRAISE FOR

AARON PHILIP CLARK

"T.S. Eliot referred to it as tradition and individual talent, the manner in which new work at once honors, builds upon, and questions what has come before. Chester Himes, Richard Wright, James Baldwin—Aaron Philip Clark has been paying attention. "
    —James Sallis, author of *CYPRESS GROVE* and *CHESTER HIMES: A LIFE*

Also by **Aaron Philip Clark**

THE SCIENCE OF PAUL
A HEALTHY FEAR OF MAN

AARON PHILIP CLARK

THE FURIOUS WAY
Text copyright © 2019 Aaron Philip Clark

Published by Shotgun Honey, an imprint of Down & Out Books

Shotgun Honey
PO Box 75272
Charleston, WV 25375
www.ShotgunHoney.com

Down & Out Books
3959 Van Dyke Rd, Ste. 265
Lutz, FL 33558
www.DownAndOutBooks.com

Cover Design by Bad Fido.

First Printing 2019

ISBN-10: 1-64396-062-8
ISBN-13: 978-1-64396-062-3

Thanks to everyone who helped me clear the hurdles.

THE FURIOUS WAY

"There's no such thing as life without bloodshed."
– Cormac McCarthy

PREFACE

LUCY RAMOS SAT ON THE EDGE of her mattress naked under her robe while a blonde boy freshened up in the bathroom. He came out trailed by a musky cologne and planted a moist kiss on her lips. He had gotten dressed, back into his tailored slacks and Italian loafers.

He was probably twenty-four with a youthful face. Lucy wasn't certain and had never cared enough to ask.

"Gotta run," he said, "see you soon?"

"Okay," Lucy said.

She was still a bit turned on and there was a half-bottle of Shiraz left. She would have asked him to stay but figured being alone would do her best—she needed time to think.

"You should probably eat something," he said as he slipped into his blazer. "I could order for you. Maybe from that Thai place you like?"

Lucy laid her head against the pillow and was silent. He stood for a moment, his wispy breathing filled the space.

"You mind blowing out the candle?" Lucy asked.

He walked over to a nightstand and picked up two one

hundred-dollar bills. He gently blew on the candle wick and the room went dark.

"Don't forget to lock the door," he said as he stumbled over Lucy's clothes. Lucy's tank top had gotten caught around his foot. He shook it off and left.

Lucy barely spoke for most of her childhood. Various doctors said her lack of speech was aligned with her psyche, some side-effect of trauma over her mother's death. It would take her years of speech therapy and shrinks to overcome the condition, but even after, she was quiet and disturbed. As a child, her doctor had diagnosed her with Asperger Syndrome—a mild form that presented in Lucy a keen memory. Her mind worked like an old VCR, she could rewind to moments in her past and recall every consequential detail— it had a way of keeping her up at night, robbing her of the ability to truly forget the fateful events in her life. And perhaps it was her quiet nature, her off-kilter way that intrigued the gigolo, the blonde boy, who went by the name Kip. She was a challenge for him. Every Tuesday night at 9:30 he would arrive inundated with virility, walking with a wide gate, upright and justified. It reminded Lucy of how John Wayne strolled about in his Westerns.

Lucy enjoyed time with Kip, but she never knew ecstasy, and this only frustrated him. She left him a browbeaten boy with all confidence shaken. Sometimes she would allow him to clean up afterwards while she stood on the balcony listening as he sung 1980s power ballads in the shower. With a cigarette clasped between her two fingers, she would overlook Los Angeles. She saw the city as a great maze of unpredictability, and this frightened her. She often couldn't walk out of her door sober and struggled not to become a complete shut-in. Kip was her connection to the outside world. She liked to listen to his ramblings. Highly animated, he'd gesture when recalling his day—the car that cut him off on Fairfax, the barista who scorched his latte, the chicken salad he gave to a homeless man on the 110 off-ramp for "good karma"—reminders of life in the city.

Twice a year, Lucy would venture outside the seven-block radius of her apartment. Usually she'd skateboard or take the bus to a museum where she could observe life in near silence. But this time Lucy had a plan—she'd take the bus to San Pedro, a port town south of Downtown. There, she would see a man who could help her make good on a promise, a blood oath that she made as a young girl.

CHAPTER ONE

THE 81 WAS THE ONLY BUS that traveled into San Pedro from downtown Los Angeles. The bus was always packed. The adage that no one walked in L.A. was true, but they damn sure rode. The bus reeked—mostly of sweat and cheap fragrances like the knock-offs peddlers sold on street corners near Lucy's apartment building.

The bus had been sitting in traffic for ten minutes. The city seemed even louder on the 110 Freeway—car horns and squeaking brakes. Even from the confines of the bus, she felt assaulted by the noise of it all. Lucy thought if the devil was real, he'd make hell an L.A. freeway and the traffic never-ending.

Lucy observed her fellow passengers. She wondered if she was missing out on things by staying in her apartment for several months straight. She rarely received paper mail; all her bills were delivered to her email account. Even her meals were delivered by the same five restaurants she had on speed dial. If she needed products she ordered from online retailers. Lucy had her groceries delivered three times a month from the closest grocery store. She wagered that if she were to die, it would possibly take weeks before anyone noticed.

Despite the loneliness, Lucy knew she was better off living a solitary life. She was in control. She didn't have to answer to anyone—not some nagging boss or manager at a retail superstore or in some office tucked away in a cubicle. She took jobs when she wanted to and spent weeks listening to vinyl records and reading books. Lucy's apartment was her haven. She was free, unlike the passengers on the bus—they were zombies. They were tired and empty husks having worked themselves to the bone like machines or the enslaved androids she read about in her Manga books. They looked real but their souls, those other worldly ghosts inside, had vacated long ago. They were dead like her mother, only her mother had decomposed in her grave—erased from the world.

Lucy never romanticized about death. In her mind, her mother didn't exist—no heaven, no hell—just gone. Lucy could accept that her mother was no more, but what bothered her was the way she left the world. When her mother was taken from her, it was as if someone had struck a match and lit Lucy on fire and she'd been burning ever since. But after twelve years she had found hope. She was on her way to San Pedro, to the home of Tito Garza. An old article in the *Los Angeles Times* had dubbed him: *El Perro of Pedro*— The Dog of San Pedro. Other news organizations coined him the *Hell Hound of Downtown* and *South Bay Butcher* because of the high volume of victims found in both areas. Garza primarily worked for the mob as a contract killer, a prolific hitman with a talent for training dogs to attack his victims. For the police, he was the stuff of nightmares—a killer who never left evidence behind, only the grisly bits of the poor schmucks he was sent to murder. Lucy hoped that Garza could still live up to the monikers and that he was every bit the killer she had read about.

The bus dropped Lucy off on Gaffey Street. She used her smart phone's GPS to navigate the rest of the way. She walked two blocks through a neighborhood that looked as if the homes were waiting to be torn down. Apartments and bungalows that were condemnable—dried and brittle stucco—structures so old they had to have been poisoning the occupants with lead or asbestos. She thought if one of the houses had ever caught fire, the entire neighborhood would burn like torch paper.

The phones' GPS alerted Lucy that she had arrived. She watched Garza's home from across the street. The lawn was in desperate need of mowing and weeds had overtaken the flowerbed. The paint was weathered and peeling; roof shingles were missing. Lucy thought that Garza likely lived alone and didn't get many visitors.

The small voice inside her head was telling her to go back home, but no amount of trepidation was going to keep her from ringing Garza's doorbell.

● ● ●

Nineteen—the number of times Tito Garza avoided prosecution, only spending ten years in the California State Penitentiary for decades of criminal acts. Now, an old man, he was weary and alone—a shadow of his former self—respected by the dead and pissed on by the living. Two days ago, the neighborhood kids stole his dog; a Chihuahua bitch he found in an alley, rain soaked and near death. He had nursed the dog back to health but now he feared she was dead and was expecting, any day, for them to throw what was left of her on his porch. If only he were twenty years—no, fifteen years younger. He'd be healthier and fit, and he could do something. When they tagged his mailbox and house, he grumbled, cursing at them from the window. Only for a group of boys to return later, painting vulgarity and what looked to be a large penis on his front door. "Little shits," he'd say, blotting out their scrawls with white paint. Garza was running out of white paint and patience.

● ● ●

There was weeks' worth of newspapers on the front porch. Lucy hadn't seen that many newspapers in years and couldn't remember the last time she had read one. She rang Garza's doorbell and listened for the chime but heard nothing. Guessing the bell might be broken; she knocked on the door and waited. Garza opened the door slowly, enough to see the skinny girl standing on his porch. Lucy struggled to get a good look at him, but most of his face was hidden behind the door. Garza studied Lucy—looking her up and down. She stood in jeans, a tank top, and slip-on gum-soled sneakers. Noticing the backpack, Garza assumed the worst.

"You got my dog in there?" he asked.

"What?"

"My dog in that bag?"

"No," Lucy said, "why would I have your dog?"

"Thought maybe you found her."

"No."

"What are you doing here if it's not about my dog?"

"Are you Tito Garza?"

Garza was silent for a moment, then he shut the door.

"I know it's you, Mister Garza."

"You a reporter?" He shouted through the door. "I gave my last interview thirty years ago, so you're wasting your time."

"I'm not a reporter."

"Then how did you find me?"

"The internet."

"Give me a fucking break." He opened the door. "You're one of those death freaks ain't you? Going around getting autographs from supposed serial killers, mobsters and shit. You people are sick, you know that? Now get the hell off my porch!"

"Mister Garza, please. I have money. I'll pay you for your time. Just talk to me."

"You bullshitting me?"

"No. I've got the cash."

"Well, you don't look like a reporter."

"I'm not. My name is Lucita—I go by Lucy."

"Fifty bucks will get you twenty minutes. I'll need to pat you down first."

"Pat me down?"

"You want in or not?"

"Okay. Fine."

Lucy was surprised by Garza's level of protest. He didn't put up as much a fuss as she thought he would. Perhaps he was so desperate for a visitor that he was willing to let anyone in? Or maybe he was so broke that any prospect of making a few bucks was worth it?

Lucy stood still in the doorway while the old man ran his hands about her body, checking for weapons or a wire. When Garza was satisfied, he let Lucy in and shut the door behind them. He took a seat in his recliner and lit a cigarette. Lucy was frozen; she didn't know whether to sit or keep standing. She looked around the house, dark and musty—absent was family photos. The house felt cold—a well-worn sofa, a recliner, a table, and a few cheap knickknacks on the mantle above the fireplace. Two dead roses that had dried but remained intact were arranged around an urn on display in a curio cabinet, along with commemorative Dodger plates. It all lacked a woman's touch and Lucy realized that she was probably the first woman in years to set foot in the dwelling.

"You gonna sit down?"

Garza gave a phlegmy cough and then pointed to the sofa. Lucy sat with her legs wide, the way she'd seen Kip do. She thought it'd give her confidence, but it didn't. She could feel the sofa's springs pushing through the fabric and she tried to adjust herself in such a way to alleviate the pressure.

"I don't get visitors," Garza said.

Lucy nodded as she continued to scan the house.

"The goddamn internet…I miss the days you could disappear for two-hundred bucks. Now, nobody is really gone until they're down in the ground," he said.

"So, you're safe here?" Lucy asked.

"Safe from what?"

"I don't know? I found you. There could be people out there—people who could mean you harm."

"I've outlived all those people. I'm an old ghost. No one is looking for me. It's been years since anybody has knocked on my door. That is until you, which is why I'm deciding whether to let you walk out of here." Garza took a long drag off the menthol. His face was expressionless. Lucy searched his eyes—nothing.

"People know I'm here," she said gently.

"Yeah? What people?"

The old man looked worn-out. But Lucy knew it could be a put on—his hunched back and shuffling feet could be hiding a deceptive strength.

"My boyfriend," she said.

"What man would let his woman knock on my door?"

"Maybe he's waiting outside and if I don't come out, he's coming in."

"Shit you say." Garza stood up and walked over to the window. He pressed back the curtain and gazed out. "Ain't nothing out there but strays."

When he turned around, Lucy stood holding pepper spray.

"I'll do it," she said.

"I bet you will."

"Don't test me, man. That's not why I came here."

"I ain't gonna hurt you. Relax."

"You don't hurt women?"

"What kind of question is that?"

"I know you don't," Lucy said, "and that's part of the code, isn't it?"

"What code?"

"The *gangster code*."

"You watch too many movies. I've seen men beat on women my whole life. Doesn't turn me on—never did. Besides, you're too green to be any trouble." Garza sat back down in the chair. "It's best to get on with it."

"I need information."

"I don't rat. I don't care how much money you've got. And that is part of the code in case you were wondering."

Lucy opened her backpack. Inside, two stacks of bills were held by rubber bands. "I'm talking more like advice—tutelage."

"What's the subject?"

"Murder."

"I look like a fool to you?"

"I'll pay you for every minute—every hour it takes to learn."

"And what exactly would you be paying me for?" He crushed the cigarette in a Dodger themed porcelain tray made to look like a baseball.

"I need you to teach me how to kill."

The old man laughed.

"I'm serious," Lucy said.

"I don't know what you've heard but I ain't no killer."

"Not anymore, maybe, but you used to be. I know all about you. I know why they call you *El Perro of Pedro*—the dog of the city."

Garza rested his head back and sighed. "I like dogs—is that a crime?"

"But we aren't talking pets and you know it."

"Loyalty, chica—dogs will do anything for you if you treat um' fair."

"Even kill a whole family for you?" Lucy asked.

Garza's mouth curled to resemble a half smile. He was impressed by how much Lucy knew about him. Sure, most of the information was easily accessible on the internet or in old articles, but she had clearly put in the time. Garza wondered how many hours she had spent researching. Had she learned enough to write a book? Writing a book would be a far safer pursuit he thought, but Garza knew that wasn't who Lucy was. He had always been good at reading people; it was a tradecraft—a well-honed skill. He was still piecing her together, but she stank of desperation and hunger.

Lucy's heartbeat sounded, fluctuating from intrigue to fear—the slow to the rapid, a fitful patter. Garza recognized the tremble in Lucy's left leg as a movement brought about by fear. And fear was necessary; it was the first step to trusting someone. The only people Garza ever worried about were those who never exhibited fear because it meant they were likely psychotic and couldn't be trusted or controlled. Though Garza knew he wasn't the picture of mental health, he never doubted his sanity. It was the cold, clamminess of fear that reminded him that he hadn't gone mad. On the contrary, killing for money was an occupational choice, and it didn't make him crazy—it made him valuable.

"How much money did you say you had?" Garza asked.

"How much do you charge?"

Lucy's question was foolish; it was the kind of question that showed Garza that she had no concept of her request. But she did have balls, enough to knock on his door—to come inside and sit a spell with a man who had slaughtered people without a second thought.

"You want me to teach you how to kill somebody like I was teaching you how to switch gears on a forklift? Who is it? Some Joe Blow who scorned you in the fifth grade? Some uncle who got too touchy feely when you were thirteen? Life ain't pretty, chica. Deal with it and move on."

"Funny coming from you," Lucy said, "word is you killed a man for spilling coffee on your pinstripes."

"You think you know me? You don't know shit from shoe shine."

"That's why I need you. I've got ten thousand. I could get more but I'd need some time."

"Don't speak, just listen," he said, "you think you're a killer? You think you've got that inside?" Garza pointed at Lucy's chest as if he could see past the flesh and bone. She felt penetrated and exposed in a way that made her stomach clinch.

Garza continued: "Next to my house there's an alley. Do you know what alley I'm speaking of?"

"Yes," Lucy said.

Garza spoke slowly and without blinking. "At the end of this alley is a house. Boys live there, about three of them, and they've taken my dog and I want it back. I don't care what you must do but if you return her to me, I will help you. Do we understand each other?"

Lucy nodded.

"I prefer you say it."

"Yes, I understand. But I have a question."

"Okay."

"What kind of dog is it?"

"It's a Chihuahua."

"Name?"

"Gazpacho."

• • •

Lucy stood at the end of the alley watching two boys drink beer and laugh on the bungalow porch. The house was old and covered in gang graffiti. She began walking toward the boys with the pepper spray in her back pocket. Her knees were stiff, and with every step she felt like she was pushing against ocean current. As she approached the boys, they seemed to ignore her. Lucy believed she was pretty but not in the way that would make the boys stutter. She was thin and thought if she ate more, she could develop curves like the girls had who teased her throughout high school—the ones who called her flat-chested and flicked gum into her hair. But no matter how much Lucy ate, her body never changed. And she didn't have a mother to tell her it was normal, to tell her that all the women in their family were built small but had big hearts and were thin but scrappy in a way that let people know not to trifle with them. No, Lucy was left to stare into a mirror where she scrutinized herself—breasts she wanted to be larger, a protruding collarbone, and a stomach with dry, white patches riddled around her naval—a condition she was told was hereditary.

Lucy hadn't changed much since high school, only she no longer gave a damn about what people thought of her appearance. She still wore too much eyeliner and stud earrings that matched the stud in her nose. Three dots were tattooed between her thumb and index finger symbolizing her three years of sobriety; though, she had long relapsed, taking to drinking wine and syrupy liquors with Kip. Lucy's thirst for hard dope had been substituted for hard sex, but it wasn't the sex that Lucy was addicted to. She craved the moments after, when Kip's hand would rest atop her hand, and she would imagine what life was like for everyday people. Lucy would never be an everyday person—she didn't know any everyday people—not Garza, not Kip, and not the gangbangers on the porch. Her mother was a dreamer. She had chased the idyllic "good life" and it had only gotten her killed. Lucy knew everyone in society had their place and her place wasn't with everyday people—the nine-to-fivers, the college co-eds, the mall shoppers. She was an outsider; ignored and unworthy of a second look. Her place was in her apartment with her books, poems, and punk rock.

"Hey girl, what you want?" a tall brown-skinned boy asked. He looked Latino and spoke with an accent. His pants were saggy, barely held up by a belt and his left hand was shoved into his pocket.

"I'm looking for a dog…a Chihuahua."

"This ain't no pound, bitch," he took a sip of beer from a long neck.

"Do you have the dog or not?"

"What if I do?"

"I'm here to take it home."

The boys laughed.

"You ain't taking shit home," he said as he set his beer on the porch step and approached Lucy.

Lucy felt for the pepper spray.

"Don't fuck with me," Lucy said.

"You're wasting your time, bitch. That dog is as dead as

14

you about to be."

The boy took a step forward and Lucy sprayed his face until he dropped to the grass and hollered. The other boy, black and wearing a baseball cap, leapt from the porch and struck Lucy against the temple with his fist. She dropped instantly and sunk into the pain. She felt a surge of darkness and then fatigue. She wanted to sleep but managed to rise, only to be hit again by two knuckles under her rib cage. The boy Lucy sprayed managed to see enough to get to his feet. He began kicking her while furiously wiping the spray from his eyes. The boys were striking steady blows with fists and feet. She couldn't get her bearings; the world was spinning. She cried, she gasped for air—she was convinced they would kill her.

Garza emerged with a metal pipe in hand. Lucy's vision had blurred but she could still see the boys being struck to the ground and bleeding from their heads. She realized that Garza still had it, that rage inside, that age nor time had cured. It boiled to the surface and with each swing the hollow metal whistled through the air. He left the boys alive but seemed to struggle with the choice—his hands tremored, and he clinched his jaw. He stood over the boy who had thrown the first blow. He watched him spit blood and teeth and wheeze, pleading for the beating to stop. Garza breathed deeply with purpose, as if to calm himself—a race engine after a drag, still idling hot. Then he helped Lucy to her feet, braced her near limp body with his shoulder, and began to walk back down the alley.

"I'm sorry," Lucy said.

"For what?"

She breathed heavy and spit globs of blood.

"I think they killed your dog."

"Ah, Lucita, you've got heart," Garza said, "I'll give you that."

CHAPTER TWO

LUCY RESTED ON THE SOFA. The bruise on her stomach had grown and darkened in hue; there was a gash in her left eyebrow. Garza gathered ice from the freezer and then wrapped it in a towel and laid it across her stomach—she flinched. He knew Lucy wouldn't need a hospital. He had seen worse injuries—broken limbs and noses, contusions, and knife wounds. Lucy wasn't coughing up blood or struggling to breathe; she just needed time to heal.

Garza gave her pills for the pain and stayed vigil. When morning came, he served her broth that she sipped from a ladle, unable to manage a spoon. Lucy didn't speak. When he wasn't watching the Dodgers, he sang softly along with Spanish ballads and Soul he played through an old radio. On the third day, there was a thump against his front door. He peered from behind the curtain and saw no one. He opened the door and found Gazpacho dead and missing her tail. The dog had been burned, scorching along her snout and paws. He wrapped the dog in a black trash bag and carried her outside to the garage. There, he put Gazpacho in the deep freezer, amongst beef patties and ice cream. He needed time to decide where to bury the pet and the freezer was best to keep away the rot. Garza always believed that Gazpacho would find him dead one morning and howl to the heavens until someone was annoyed enough to come around. He'd be found in his boxer shorts, a photo of his dear Maria on his nightstand, lying with his head against the pillow or his body sprawled on his bedroom floor. The police would be called, and photos would be taken. An investigation would be necessary to rule out foul play, but it would be of natural causes—a stroke, a heart-attack, something that transpired in his sleep. It depressed him to think of his death that way. After all he had done and survived, he didn't want to die in San Pedro, alone, with only a dog to mourn him.

• • •

With the old man's help, Lucy sat up with a pillow propped behind her back. She lifted her shirt slightly to see the condition of her bruise. She ran her fingers over her stomach and ribs; there was a greasy film.

"What did you put on me?"

"Ice…some ointment."

"All you saw was my stomach, right?"

"Yes. So, what's with the sores on your skin? You sick or something?"

"I'm not sick."

"I knew a guy with Lupus—it looks like Lupus."

"It isn't Lupus and it's nothing contagious."

"You have that your whole life?"

"Yes," Lucy said.

"Shit."

"So, did you get your dog?"

Garza scowled. "Dead like you said."

"Damn."

"Can you walk?"

"I can try."

Lucy stood up. Pain shot across her abdomen. She wanted to cry but couldn't in front of Garza. She took a few steps toward the door, then walked back and leaned against the edge of the sofa. Never had she felt the type of pain caused by the beating—never had she been that close to death, and strangely, it made her feel even more alive.

"Who's Rita?" Garza asked.

"What?"

"You kept saying Rita in your sleep."

"My mother," Lucy said with a quiver.

Garza lit a smoke.

"I'm sure that boyfriend is searching for you about now."

"I haven't had a boyfriend since thirteen," she said.

"You a dyke or something?"

"WTF, man?"

"What the hell is *WTF*?"

"What-the-fuck?"

"Then why not say that?" Garza asked.

"Not that it matters but no."

"Then what's your hang-up?"

"I don't date."

"A lady should never date, she should be courted."

"I don't court then."

"Where did all that money come from?"

"I saved it."

"You work?"

Garza thumbed the cigarette ash into the tray.

"Yes."

"Doing what?"

"I'd rather not say."

"Who's coming to get you? You have friends or something?"

"I can manage on the bus," Lucy said, "I guess this means you're not going to help me?"

Garza took a final drag and then pressed the cigarette butt into the tray.

"Go home," he said blowing a reserve of smoke into the air.

"Is it because I got beat?"

"No," he said, "you did your best. It was shit but it was your best."

"Is it because I couldn't save her, Gazpacho?"

"No, that isn't on you. That's on me. They should have never gotten her in the first place. I fucked up."

"So, I got my ass kicked for nothing?"

"You needed it and I needed to know..."

"Know what? And what the hell do you mean I needed it?"

"Maybe you want to kill too much. It makes you sloppy—too much emotion, too much hunger ain't good when it comes to killing."

"That's why I need you. You can teach me to shut it all out."

"I can't teach you that. No one can."

"I'm begging you."

"And what terrible thing did this person do, huh? What would make you risk flushing your life down the shitter?"

"He murdered my mother."

"Mothers die every day, what makes yours' any different?"

Lucy's dead mother was a raw nerve always exposed. She wore her pain like a merit badge, as if it were something earned that needed to be gazed upon. The old man saw this as a weakness and something that needed to be purged. He knew what she didn't, that empathy, sympathy, love or hate, had no place when it came time to kill. The work required indifference. Feelings could be blinding, and Garza had to be able to see shit coming ten miles out.

"Fuck this. I'll deal with it myself," she said.

"You can't even manage two punks."

"Go to hell."

Lucy heaved the backpack of cash over her shoulder with a painful grunt. Garza watched her intensely—she was broken but he felt nothing. He had no allegiance to Lucy, she was nobody. Her dead mother was nobody. All he could think about was his dog lying in the freezer. Was she alive when they cut off her tail and burned her? Did she suffer? Of course, she suffered. She was so defenseless, a sweet lap dog that had never faced the kind of cruelness the boys who tortured her possessed. But Garza was all too familiar with that brand of malevolence; it had taken residence in his heart for as long as he could remember—but it had fallen dormant.

And as for the girl, fearless or stupid? Maybe she welcomed death? Garza wasn't sure. He wondered if she could be useful. Maybe a resurrection was in order and he would start with the boys who killed his Gazpacho.

"Put the bag down," Garza said.

Lucy faced him.

"I'll take half now—five grand."

"Okay."

"You've bought yourself two weeks," he said, "come back here once you've healed up."

"Two weeks for five grand?"

"Did I stutter?"

"Okay."

"But get one thing straight. If you get pinched, it's on you. You don't mention my name—not a damn word. You never were here. You don't even know me. Got it?"

"Yeah, I got it."

"Good."

"For what it's worth, I'm sorry about your dog," she said.

"Your first lesson—don't be."

• • •

Lucy walked out of the house and headed back toward Gaffey Street. The sun was bright and each time she passed a car, she caught her reflection in its windows. She gnashed her teeth at the thought the boys had nearly killed her. But when she considered what she had accomplished, she couldn't help but smile with satisfaction. She may have looked and felt like day-old deli meat, but she was one step closer to making good on her promise.

CHAPTER THREE

WHEN LUCY ARRIVED at her apartment the night was fresh. She was tired and aching from the beating. As she approached her front door, Kip appeared in black leather and denim. His hair was slicked back, and his jeans were shoved down into leather combat boots. She thought how ridiculous he looked—a "Ken" doll with outfits for various occasions— tonight he was a 50's throwback with a touch of hipster. Lucy wanted to laugh, but the pain of such an act steadily out- weighed the want, and she settled for pretending he wasn't there.

"Where the hell have you been?" he asked, "I've been call- ing and calling. I thought something happened to you."

Lucy entered her apartment and collapsed on the bed. Kip stood in the doorway, his thumbs shoved into his pockets.

"Are you really going to lay there and ignore me?" He walked into the apartment and shut the door behind him.

Lucy got up from the bed and began to take off her clothes, not giving thought to her bruises. When Kip saw them, he gasped. Lucy quickly put her back to him.

"Turn around," Kip demanded.

She hesitated for a moment, and then a kind of pride came over her and she turned to face him. She had survived a fight, a beating, one that had her outnumbered and could have been the end of her. She wanted him to gaze upon her as proof that she was not some meek girl who needed codling and pity—some pathetic thing that had to pay for intimacy and menial conversation. She was more than that, much more. She was something Kip would never understand.

"What the hell happened to you? You need to get to the hospital or something. Come on, I can drive you."

Kip took her by the arm and tried to pull her toward him. Lucy jerked away and spit in his face.

"You bitch! Are you crazy?" he cried.

"Leave! Leave now and don't ever come back," she said.

"You're fucking nuts, you know that?"

She ushered Kip out, swatting at his face. He was still wiping the saliva from his cheek and cursing when she slammed the door. He pounded in protest.

"Fuck off, Kip," Lucy said, "I'll call the cops—I mean it."

Kip retreated at the mention of the police.

Later, Lucy drew a bath and sat in the water for a long while, letting the warmth wash against the bruises. After, she rubbed coco butter on her stomach, put on an oversized T-shirt, and climbed into bed. Her mind was busy as she lied awake for hours recounting the beating and how Garza had cared for her. Finally, her eyes gave way and she drifted to sleep.

When she woke, it was late morning. The sun was hazy—the smog heavy—and the smell of the corner panaderia wafted through her window. Hunger had set in. The bruises were still tender; still dark.

She poured a glass of orange juice, toasted a bagel and

watched the downtown skyline. She wondered how people could live in such a city that seemed destined to fail—reduced to rubble by an earthquake— "the big one"—or overtaken by a rising Pacific. Yet, somehow, people got up every morning, got dressed, made breakfast, kissed their families, and went to work knowing that at any moment it could all be over—that Los Angeles was too good to be true, too idyllic to remain—too beautiful a starlet to stay alive, and would have to die someday. And there would be no one left to mop up the floor; a ravaged city home to nothing but sun and palms, and the dead, who wouldn't mind at all.

Lucy spent most of the day in bed, reading and listening to vinyl records. She ordered in Thai, and then drafted her last Will and Testament. She would donate most of her belongings to the group home she was raised in. She didn't have much that held value, rather it was sentiment—items that helped her through difficult times growing up—her collection of Grunge and Punk recordings, the writings of Kris Krause, and her antique Ferrania Ibis. When she was done, she sealed the Will in an envelope and placed it in her desk drawer where it would be easy to find in the event of her demise. Lucy felt free—she understood there were only two results of carrying out her oath—prison or death. There wasn't much chance of her coming out clean. And the latter thrilled her, she was eager to get on with it—the *after*. As for prison, she saw it as an inconvenience that wouldn't be much different from her life now. She thought if the worst things that could happen to a person were prison and death, then she truly had nothing left to fear.

The following day, Lucy felt well enough to make the bus trip back to San Pedro. When she arrived at Garza's home, the old man had just woken up. He greeted her in boxer shorts and bed slippers. His bare chest was speckled with gray hair and a scar that resembled railroad tracks, extended across his belly. He braced his right hand against the door post. Despite his age and tendency to hunch, he still had considerable muscle tone. His arms were defined and there was a visible tightness in his upper body.

"And here you are," he said smugly while scratching his chest.

"Yes."

"How's the bruise?"

"Better."

He grunted with approval. "Come in."

He moved aside, letting Lucy past. She took a seat on the sofa.

"Hungry? I was about to cook up some eggs and bacon."

"No, I'm fine."

"TV works. I ain't got cable but you can get three or four channels with those rabbit ears."

"I don't watch TV."

"Not even the Dodgers?"

"Don't care much about sports."

Lucy sat quietly in the living room as Garza shuffled about in the kitchen, knocking pots around until he found his skillet. He cracked two eggs and whipped them in a bowl. He added butter to the hot skillet, and then poured the eggs. When the eggs were firm, he lowered two slices of bacon into the cast iron.

"Can you drive?" he asked loudly from the kitchen.

"No license," Lucy shouted back.

"But you know how, don't you?"

"Took the bus all my life."

"My van is on the fritz and I'm going to need you to help me get it up and running."

"I don't know shit about cars," she said.

"You ain't got to know. I just need your eyes."

The old man plated his food and carried it over to the sofa. He sat down and ate, while Lucy looked on.

"You don't eat much, do you?" Garza asked.

"I eat plenty."

"Don't look like it. You're not one of them anorexics, are you? I hear that's a big thing now with the girls."

"No. I'm not." Lucy glared. "How old do you think I am?"

"I don't know? How old do you think I am?"

"You're eighty-two. Like I said, I did my research."

"I'd say you look about seventeen."

"I'm twenty-two—old enough to drink, old enough to buy a gun and old enough to gamble."

"And old enough to go to the chair."

"California doesn't have an electric chair—never did. It's lethal injection or gas."

"It's a saying," he said, shoving eggs into his mouth. "Besides, dead is dead no matter how you get there."

"Where did you come from anyway?" she asked, "Before you came to San Pedro, I mean?"

"I thought you knew everything about me? Everything that damn internet tells you anyways."

"It mentioned New York and Jersey, and then things went cold...until you ended up in Los Angeles. So, what were you, Mickey Cohen's pool boy—the kid who poured his Schnapps, or did you shine Siegel's shoes?"

"It was a lifetime ago. And let's get something straight, this is a business arrangement—plain and simple. I'm not some fucking school project so enough with the questions."

"Sure. Whatever. What are we doing today?"

"Today we bury my perro," he said, consuming the last bit of eggs and bacon. He carried his plate to the sink and ran it under hot water. "I'll get washed up. Then we'll get started."

● ● ●

The old van took up most of the space in Garza's garage. Outside of the deep freezer, there wasn't room for much else. Lucy poked about, peeking into boxes of keepsakes and old black and whites. Photos of a young Garza, who seemed like a different man, short in stature but with a solid build and a pointed chin which was now veiled by unkempt hair. His face was still taut—thickened by repeated poundings and fractures. But what had been gone for years was his wavy black hair, cropped and parted to the left. The current Garza was a balding sap hunched over the van's engine, mumbling to himself as he wiped his oily hands against faded polyester.

Lucy nudged a box marked "Maria" with her foot. She quickly bent down as if to tie her shoe and pulled back on the cardboard flap. A cream wedding dress sealed in plastic was inside, along with baby shoes that had been bronzed. There was a framed photo of Garza standing with a woman. A young boy clung to his leg; his face was partially obscured as he shied away from the camera.

"Give me a hand," asked Garza, "pass me that socket wrench from the toolbox."

"What does it look like?"

"You don't know what a socket wrench is?"

"I wouldn't be asking if I did."

He lifted his head from over the engine and walked over to the toolbox where he exhibited the wrench for Lucy. "This is a socket wrench," he said.

"Who's Maria?" Lucy asked.

"You got some stones, you know that?"

"Just curious."

"Don't be."

"Was she your wife?"

Garza sighed. "Yes."

"And the boy?"

"What do you think?"

"Your son?"

"And before you ask, they're dead. I wouldn't suggest you push for the details, not with this wrench in my hand."

Lucy moved away from the box. "I just never thought you had a family."

"We weren't married long—a couple of years. We were both young and I was a nobody."

"Makes sense. There wasn't any mention of it online. It doesn't really fit the profile, though."

"If I told you I can dance a mean Samba, would that be part of the profile?"

"I don't know."

"Profiles are bullshit, always have been. Besides, it wasn't until later that I realized that having a family didn't fit with my line of work."

"They were taken from you, weren't they? Is that when you started training the dogs?"

"The things I love tend to get taken away. Probably why Gazpacho is in that freezer."

"You some kind of profiler or something?"

"No, but your profile is online. Someone posted it in one of those police forums—it's gotten thousands of hits."

"So?"

"It was all textbook—narcissistic personality disorder, anti-social, prone to irrational violence, and a gross inability to empathize."

"Hand me the flashlight. You do know what that looks like, right?"

Lucy pulled the black Maglite from the toolbox and handed it to Garza. "Still can't see worth a damn," he said, "I need you to look for any oil drips when I start her up."

"Okay."

Garza reached over the wheel and turned the key. Lucy was bent over the engine. She could feel the heat and could smell burning but saw no oil.

"Anything dripping?" Garza asked.

"No."

"Good," he said cutting the engine.

"Now what?"

"Take Gazpacho out of the freezer and put him in the van."

Garza went into the house while Lucy rummaged in the freezer, trying to get a good grip on the dog which was frozen solid. Once she got a hold, she quickly carried Gazpacho to the van and laid her on the metal floor amongst a shovel and pick. The van was ancient to Lucy, and it smelled of beer and cigarettes. When Garza returned, he was dressed in pressed slacks, a crisp dress shirt and fedora. His wingtips were buffed shiny and he held the dog's collar in his hand.

"Let's go," he said.

Lucy got into the van and buckled herself. Garza didn't bother with such things; it was the least of his worries. He didn't have auto insurance or a valid driver's license. He did, however, have a small snub-nosed pistol in his right pocket and extra bullets in his left—an old habit that would never die.

The van had limited horsepower and a failing clutch. Garza worked the gearbox the best he could but at times he was unable to catch third, and let it hang in second. The frozen dog slid across the van's floor—a loud thump sounded when Garza stopped at red lights and stop signs. The inertia sent the dog careening forward and then swiftly to the rear.

"What kind of van is this?" she asked.

"It's a 63' Econoline."

"As in 1963? Damn, this is like vintage or something."

"What the hell do you mean vintage?"

"Like a throwback, you know? Like an antique."

"It's no antique." He pulled down the sun visor.

• • •

San Pedro was an old town, and it was the kind of place a person stumbled upon by accident. It was the end of Los Angeles; the last stop after the 110 Freeway where drivers were deposited onto Gaffey Street—a busy stretch that ended at the Pacific Ocean. The town felt distant—removed from everything, and Lucy understood why Garza had retired there. The bars were full of drunks and the alleys with vagrants, and nobody asked questions. A man could drive around aimlessly without the proper credentials and a dead dog, and if he obeyed the traffic laws nobody noticed.

"So where are we going? A pet cemetery or something?" she asked.

Garza didn't answer. He seemed deep in thought. Focused on what? Lucy couldn't imagine. He was hard to read sometimes; his body language betrayed his words. The conversation could be benign, but he'd be tense, shoulders tight and hunched—ready to pounce.

They drove on for another ten minutes toward the beaches. The dog thumped, the clutch burned, and Lucy stared out of the window at the passersby's wondering if the old man was really going to teach her what she needed to know about killing, or had she blown her savings on a has-been? He had yet to show her anything worthwhile and she was getting anxious; she needed a sign that Garza still knew what the hell he was doing.

The van pulled into the parking lot at Cabrillo Beach.

Garza got out. Lucy hesitated for a moment but followed when Garza tapped his finger against her window and cut her a look that reminded her of his volatile nature.

"Get the dog. I'll carry the shovel," he said.

Lucy picked up the dog and followed Garza down to the beach.

"Please don't tell me you're planning to bury this dog on the beach?"

"Most Chihuahuas hate the water. That little shit couldn't get enough."

"The sand—you're burying him in the sand?" she asked, "You'll get fined."

"It's the goddamn earth, nobody owns it."

"Yeah, but…"

"You'd be better off if you gave less of a damn," he said driving the shovel into the sand. He began to dig; the sand collected on his wingtips and blew against his slacks. He had picked the most secluded part of beach he could find, but it was not without onlookers. A young girl and her mother sat a few feet away under an umbrella. The little girl was building a sandcastle and was looking to her mother for encouragement as it threatened to crumble. But her mother was preoccupied, watching the burial of Gazpacho.

"People are looking at us," Lucy said.

"Put him in the hole."

Lucy lowered the dog into the hole and took a step back. The old man took off his fedora, knelt, and placed the dog's collar on its body which hadn't fully thawed. He held it there a moment and then rose from the sand. With the back of the shovel, he pushed the accumulated sand over the carcass.

"Let's go," he said putting his fedora back on.

The old man was quiet as they drove back down Gaffey. Lucy couldn't keep her eyes off him. It was the first time she had really looked at him—had truly seen him, not as the Perro of Pedro, but as a human being—flawed, yes, but human. And she considered the possibility that Gazpacho was the only thing left in the world that he gave a damn about, and she knew in that moment that the boys in the shabby house would soon be dead.

• • •

The animal shelter was in the neighboring Harbor City. It once was a house but had been converted to care for dogs and cats. The larger breeds were kept outside. There were paths to walk but the kennels consumed much of the backyard. A small area was designated for bathing and grooming, and each dog had a chew toy and bowls for water and food. But it was a prison and it was where most of the dogs would die. Those who wouldn't be adopted would be put down for being undesirables. It was a game of chance, Lucy thought. Their lives, their futures, were all determined on the right person or family walking in. A connection would have to be made, one that was instant. It was something Lucy could relate to; it was her life in the foster care system, and instead of a homely shelter attendant with matted blonde hair and shit stained pants, she had a case worker named Gloria.

When Lucy was introduced to potential parents, she'd wear her nicest dress—blue and white laced; her hair would be curled, and she never chewed gum. These were the three things Gloria mandated, and Lucy believed that if she did these things it would give her a fighting chance, and that someone would see how great a kid she was. But Lucy never made a connection with a family, not one that lasted anyway. And on her 18th birthday she left the foster home, got an apartment and began to seek out her mother's killer. No one came to save Lucy, and no one was coming to save these dogs.

It was the way of the world—birth then death, and the happenings in-between. And Garza's chosen dogs would soon get a lesson in the in-between. They'd have one purpose—to be his soldiers and to carry out his commands.

"Any particular breed you're interested in?" asked the shelter attendant.

"We'll know it when we see it," Lucy said.

"We haven't had too many visitors this week. They're kind of starved for attention. If one catches your eye, let me know and I'll make the proper introduction."

The phone rang, and the attendant excused herself, leaving Garza and Lucy to inspect the dogs more closely. Garza knelt in front of the cages. One by one, he'd stare into a dog's eyes. A weak dog would cower and withdraw into the far corner of the cage. But a dog worth its salt wouldn't back down, it would lunge, and growl and the cage would be the only thing keeping it from ripping out Garza's throat. And that would be the sign he needed—a dog governed by its instincts.

"What about this guy," Lucy asked, pointing at a chocolate Labrador. Lucy put her hand against the cage. The dog licked and panted.

"Labs are no good."

"Why?"

"It's their temperaments."

"Lovers not fighters?"

"Yes."

"How will you know when you've found the right one?"

"I look for the ones that'll do anything to be free of their cage—free of this place."

When the attendant returned, she seemed beside herself. "I apologize. We have a few dogs coming in that we may have to put down. It's not our finest hour."

"What's wrong with them?" Lucy asked.

"They've been removed from a breeder for suspected dog fighting. Most won't be adoptable, especially not for families with children. So, they'll be put down."

"But some can be adopted?" asked Garza.

"We don't know. Not yet, anyway. They'll need to be assessed."

"Assessed? How long does that take?"

"We have to check them for injuries and other health conditions. Then we'll need to see how well they react to being around the other dogs in the kennel—see if they exhibit any violent behavior."

"How long?"

"A couple of hours at the least but it could be days. But I must warn you. These dogs won't be without problems. Maybe you should consider what we have? There are some sweet dogs in the kennel, sir. Some that would make great companions."

"When will the dogs be here?"

"There's a very pleasant Beagle we call Norman."

"How long?"

"The driver is on his way—fifteen minutes or so."

"We'll wait."

"But sir…"

"We'll wait."

CHAPTER FOUR

"DOGS AREN'T THAT MUCH DIFFERENT from humans," Garza explained as he and Lucy pulled the two Pit Bulls from the back of the van. "They need things the same as humans do. My father liked dogs. He looked after a stray when I was a boy. It was old, tired and close to death. He'd pick ticks off its ears with tweezers and the ones that burrowed too deep into the dog's flesh, he'd set fire to them with a lighter till they popped. He'd rub that dog's belly; all covered in nubs and boils. I was sick by the sight of that dog. It was pathetic to see that old mutt clinging to life like that. I wanted it to die. But not my father, he'd give it baths and feed it when we barely had food ourselves. Most days he treated that dog better than me, even up until it died."

"What happened to it?" Lucy asked.

"It came around one day coughing up yellow with a little blood. It was unable to keep anything down. My father said it was dying—said it was best not to let it suffer. Before that day, I had never tasted blood that wasn't mine."

"He killed it?"

"I was standing too close when the gun went off—caught the dog's blood in my mouth."

Garza and Lucy led the dogs into the backyard. They were growling and nipping at each other. The white Pit displaying moderate aggression; it lunged at the other dog and jerked its head wildly trying to break free of the chain around its neck. Garza took up the slack in the chain and anchored the white Pit to a stake in the ground. Its coat was pristine, hardly evident of a fighting dog. Maybe it had been in a scuffle or two, but nothing serious. It was small and likely used in sparring. Or maybe it hadn't had its day yet—hadn't gotten its taste for blood. The other Pit's coat was marbled: brown, tan, black. It walked with a slight buckle in its hind quarters. Garza suspected its leg had been broken some time ago and had healed poorly. Its ears had been gnawed to gristle like skirt steak pounded thin. He chained each dog to large concrete blocks, running the chains through the block's opening until the chains were wrapped tight.

"You going to make them mean now?" Lucy asked.

"They're already mean."

"Yeah but they're not killers, not the way we want."

"How do you figure I make them into killers then?"

"I don't know. I heard people feed them gunpowder, take garden hoses to them."

"They've had enough of that. Doing it more ain't going to do shit but make them more loco. And a loco dog is a useless dog."

"How are you going to do it then?"

"Go to the kitchen. In the box are bones wrapped in foil, bring them to me."

"The box?"

"The fridge," he said.

Lucy went into the house. Garza stood watching as the

dogs sniffed about and occasionally made runs, only to be jerked back by the chains around their necks. They were strong, but the chains held. He couldn't have the dogs kill each other before morning; he needed to bond them.

Lucy returned with the pack of bones and Garza fed them to the dogs. He filled two buckets with water and the dogs drank, lopping the water for long stretches as if their thirsts could not be quenched. When they finally got their fill, they settled with the bones between their paws and ground them down. White foam collected on dark gums, as they sucked air through their snouts.

"Let them be," Garza said, "Tomorrow we begin."

He chained the gate with link and a lock. It was getting dark.

"I should get home," Lucy said.

"How come you ain't got a car but you got all that money?" Garza asked. "You could get a *chatarra*, a run-about, for a couple hundred. You wouldn't be taking the buses with all those locos and perverts."

"I never needed a car before. Never had any place to go."

"I thought you said you had a job?"

"I work from home—online."

"Doesn't anybody go to real jobs anymore?"

"Don't know. This is the most I've been away from my apartment."

Garza sighed.

"You can take the sofa, if you want."

Lucy looked to the sofa. Remembering the discomfort, she rubbed her lower back with her palm. She thought not having to return to her apartment would make life easier, but the sofa wasn't her bed. It wasn't the comfort of home.

"Don't think too long," he said. "The sofa has always served me fine but I ain't forcing it."

She was rather surprised by Garza's offer. He had gone to painstaking lengths to be left alone, and now he had offered up his home—access to what many shrinks, cops, and journalists dreamed of—the lion's den that no longer inhabited an unbridled miscreant but a circumspect man—a killer in twilight.

"Any extra blankets?" she asked.

"In the cabinet."

She took a quilt and blanket and laid them over the sofa's worn coils. Then she pressed against them, testing for comfort. She folded another blanket and made a palette. Satisfied, she laid down, her head propped against the sofa's edge.

"Night," she said.

The old man faded quietly into the hallway.

● ● ●

Lucy woke early, as the sun rose and broke through the sheer drapes. She stood at Garza's bedroom door. She could hear snoring and gently turned the knob, opening the door enough to see the man sleeping on his back. He slept straight and stiff, as if mounted to a board. He looked peculiar, as if he were awaiting surgery on an operating table. The room was dark and pungent; the sour was strong. It desperately needed airing out, and for light to be let in. The lone window was nailed shut and the glass was covered with newspaper and tape, muting sunlight to gray. A collection of small steel-belted radios occupied one bedside table, and a gooseneck lamp set on the other. The walls were worn to primer. His left hand was shoved into his boxer shorts, he was holding himself, and resting on his pillow was a picture of Maria.

Lucy watched his chest rise and fall. Then she pulled the door shut and returned to the sofa. She couldn't fall back asleep, so she sat and waited for the old man to wake.

Each day she was growing more anxious facing the task in front of her. Soon it would be time for the first cut, but Lucy didn't want to be the one tasked to work the blade. The boys in the shabby house had beaten her badly, but still, she couldn't imagine killing them. She hated this about herself— this compassion, the humanity. She wanted to purge it; to leave it behind for good.

Garza came out of his room. He scratched his chest and lit a smoke. Standing over Lucy, he took a puff and then let the cigarette burn. When the smoke was a quarter of ash dangling and begging to be flicked, he spoke: "Don't ever come into my room again."

Lucy was quiet. Even if she could string a few words together, she wouldn't know what to say. Garza stood watching the back of her head. Maybe he had forgotten he had lit the smoke? Maybe he was fixated on choking her?

"My room ain't for snooping, you understand?"

She nodded.

"Good. Now get dressed. I'll make breakfast." Garza went into the kitchen to start on breakfast. He pulled eggs and bacon from the fridge. Lucy went into the bathroom to get washed up. Garza had left a set of towels for her on the sink and a bar of soap. The white of the tub had chipped away in its center, underneath was rust and gray. It was an old soaking tub—pedestal legs and a deep basin. There was no showerhead, only an arching spout and two knobs for hot and cold. Lucy plugged the tub and began running water. She could smell bacon cooking. The smell of meat usually caused her to lose her appetite, but even her disdain for cooking flesh couldn't ease her hunger pains and her stomach's deep growls.

She got dressed; she would need to wash her clothes soon or purchase new ones. But something about wearing them made her feel good; she thought of her clothes as the uniform of a soldier. They were evidence of what she had done—and like her bruise, a tangible reminder that she was changing into something new to be reckoned with.

Lucy took a seat at the table. Garza spooned eggs onto her plate, along with three slices of bacon. "Eat. You're going to need your strength for what we have to do."

"What is it we have to do?" she asked.

"Just eat."

Lucy stared at the food and tried to imagine it in her mouth. She moved the eggs with her fork, pushing them to the plate's edge and then to the center. They were hard from sitting too long and greasy from butter. She sprinkled them with salt and pepper, the way Garza had, and brought the fork to her lips. Looking at the firm yellow clumps, she tried to bring the food closer to her mouth.

"Might be a little cold," Garza said, "I ain't got a microwave, so they'll have to do."

"It's fine."

"Then why aren't you eating it? Want toast or something?"

"I'm a vegan."

"A what?"

"I don't eat meat or dairy products."

"Then what the hell do you eat?"

"Other things."

"And what happens if you eat that bacon?"

"I don't know. I just can't."

"Is it a religious thing?"

"No."

"Then you can eat the bacon."

"I told you I'm a vegan."

"I heard you," Garza said chomping on a bacon slice. "Now this is maple cured and thick cut. It ain't cheap and it's on your plate."

"I can't."

"You mean you won't."

"What are you trying to do?" Lucy asked, "I explained the situation."

"The situation," he repeated, "a situation is watching a pal get shot and then having to dig the bullet out from under tendon. A situation is stitching up your stomach after some punk tries to gut you with a straight razor. Eating bacon is not a fucking situation. It's a choice—to eat or not to fucking eat."

"Come on—are you being serious right now?"

"You're going to put that bacon in your mouth. You're going to chew it. And you're going to swallow it."

"The hell I am!"

Garza slid his chair away from the table and quickly stood up. He took a long knife from a chopping block and placed it on the table.

"It's just bacon."

"It's more than that," he said, "you and your sensibilities—your little rules. It's carry-over from that bubble you've been living in. There's going to be things you're gonna do that you ain't gonna like. Eating bacon and eggs is the least of your worries. You don't eat meat. You say that it's murder. Give me a fucking break. Try cutting off a guy's fingertips with a steak knife—like sawing into cold sausages. You better get used to doing shit you don't want to do."

Lucy picked up the bacon. The meat was tough and sticky from the maple. She put it in her mouth and chewed. The fat like rubber—the meat salty and sweet; then, once broken down she swallowed hard. It nearly came up, but she forced it back. She tried not to think of what she had done. For most of her life, she had avoided meat, dairy, and anything that came from an animal's hide. She ate what was offered in the group homes, so she wouldn't go hungry. But once on her own, she made the rules—and she couldn't justify killing something so defenseless just for her own satisfaction.

Looking at the plate, still with two slices of bacon and a mound of eggs, she thought about the implicit nature of what she was becoming—the hypocrisy. She was no longer Lucy—vegan, cyber investigator, who donated to Greenpeace, and does no harm. Garza was right; she had been in a bubble. To hell with it, she thought.

She pushed the eggs into her mouth and after three spoonful's, they were gone. She quickly finished the bacon with her eyes closed. And for a moment, she wished she were elsewhere—maybe back in her apartment listening to Kip sing out of tune. But those thoughts soon died and when she opened her eyes, Garza had the knife in his hand and a smirk on his face.

"It didn't kill you," he said.

"I feel sick."

"Get used to it."

"What were you going to do with that?" Lucy asked. Her eyes were on the blade.

"The question is what are you going to do with it. See, we're in this now—together. There's no turning back. There's only two ways out—you kill your mark, or you end this right now." Garza grabbed Lucy's wrist. "You take this knife and you finish what you started."

Garza's thumb touched the raised, horizontal scar at the base of Lucy's palm. It was thin, somewhat superficial, and left behind by a paring knife. "I was young and stupid," she said.

"Doesn't matter…we've all got them."

"My therapist at the group home said they remind us, not

define us." Lucy chuckled. "Kinda corny, I guess."

"Whatever works," he said, "a scar ain't nothing but proof you can heal. As long as you're still around to tell about it—that's what matters."

"We should see about the dogs," Lucy said.

Garza nodded.

In the backyard, the dogs had dug holes and the white Pit had worked the chain so much, it had rubbed the skin around his neck raw. Garza gave the dogs fresh water and stale bread.

"Do you think we should name them?" Lucy asked.

"Makes sense."

Lucy approached the white Pit Bull. Studying it with her arms crossed and right hip cocked, she said, "Paco. He looks like a Paco."

Garza nodded and fed Paco more bread. Lucy approached the other dog. It growled. Lucy froze. "Shit. He's feisty."

"We'll call him, Sarge," Garza said.

"Sarge? Really?"

"He's the leader. We train him right and the other will fall in line."

"Okay. Sarge it is," Lucy said, "now what?"

"We're going to need the suit."

● ● ●

The suit was fashioned from pillows, a scuba vest, duct tape, and a surfer's wet suit. It included a goal tender's hockey mask, gloves, and leg padding. Garza had gathered most of the materials from a used sporting goods store. Lucy could barely walk with it all on. It took all her strength not to topple over.

"Why do I have to wear this thing?" she asked.

"I'm too old," Garza said, "Now, you're going to need to

listen to me carefully. I'm going to let one dog go at a time. Do not run or panic. That suit will protect all the important areas."

"All my body parts are important."

"It's the only way. They need to get it out of their systems. Only then we'll be able to teach them something."

"How long do I have to wear this thing?"

"As long as it takes," Garza said, releasing Paco. The dog B-lined toward Lucy, who had buckled at the knees and was breathing heavily. Paco took hold of her left leg, sinking his teeth into the padding. Lucy was knocked to the ground. She tried to stay calm—tried to remind herself that once the dog tired, it would be over. Paco jerked his head back and forth and pulled at her leg. The padding was beginning to give way, she could feel the wet suit exposed.

"The fucker is biting through," she said. "Get him off me!"

"He's gassing out." Garza said looking at his watch, clocking Paco's attack from the moment he had let him go. The dog grunted and pulled at Lucy's leg. It was strong enough to drag her a few inches, before releasing her in frustration. Paco was done, and Garza was pleased.

"Three lousy minutes—too damn long," he said marching over to Lucy and helping her up. Garza chained Paco, avoiding a few lackadaisical nips at his arm from the spent dog. "He's out of shape but he's got heart."

"I'm glad I was able to help you find that out."

"Relax, chica. You did well." Garza gave Paco bread and rubbed his head, telling him how great a dog he was. The dog seemed to bask in it. It was likely the first time in a long while that a human had shown some compassion toward him. In that moment, Garza knew Paco was on his way— soon, the dog would be part of their pack.

Sarge had watched Paco and Lucy, intently—never once

barking or showing any signs of aggression. The difference between him and Paco was clear. Sarge had reached his prime, he had lost too many fights and had he not been rescued from the fighting ring, he would be dead. Dogs like him could stand to lose a fight or two, but with the injuries he had sustained, he was bordering on useless. Paco was new blood—probably being groomed to take his place. Garza figured he had saved them both—one from certain death, the other from a life of suffering. It was clear, both dogs had seen their share of pain—which was inevitable—but maybe they deserved a little retribution. They had been tormented in the worst ways, and they were due a little payback. Humans are callous, worse than callous, vicious. Garza knew this better than anyone, and Lucy understood this as well. They were better off with the dogs—humans were without regard, relegated to be kings of the jungle because they evolved to walk upright. But they were more animal than any dog Garza had met.

"I have to pee," Lucy said, "I need outta this suit."

"Okay, we'll take thirty minutes. Then it's Sarge's turn."

Lucy went into the house to change. Garza rubbed against Paco's stomach and the sweet spot behind his right ear. After a few minutes, Lucy returned to the backyard, still in the suit and holding the helmet.

"Someone's at the door," she said in a whisper.

"What?"

"Someone's at the door." This time she was louder, realizing Garza couldn't stand to hear a whisper.

"Well, who the hell is it?"

"A woman. I think she may be selling something."

"Like an Avon lady?"

"I don't know. She's a white lady in a jogging suit."

"Jogging suit?" he said walking into the garage. "Stay in here."

"Fine but make it quick. I need help getting this shit off."

Garza went to the front door and looked through the peephole. A woman, blonde and in a pink velour jogging suit, stood holding a basket of baked goods in plastic wrap. He unlatched the chain and opened the door.

"Hello neighbor," she said in a bubbly voice. She wore violet eye shadow and fingernail polish that matched the velour. She looked as if she had ventured off course from some far-off place like the Valley—Tarzana or Encino.

Garza hated the Valley—the cops were the worst out there—especially if you were Mexican. Garza remembered going over the hill, slipping out of North Hollywood on a job. He rarely felt on edge, only down in the Valley and when he stood outside Maria's door, awaiting her answer—hoping she hadn't learned the truth, that he wasn't a driver or chauffeur, but instead, a killer. Maria came from a good family and her father owned a pawn shop. Maria was educated, beautiful, and always out of reach until one day she wasn't.

It would be a few years later, long after the wedding bells stopped ringing, that Maria would come to know who she had truly married.

"Yes?" Garza asked.

"We just moved into the neighborhood and I thought I'd come over and introduce myself. I'm Tina Barnes."

"Jorge's old place?"

"That's right. My husband and I are sprucing it up. We represent the Phoenix Group. Maybe you've heard of us?" Tina handed Garza a brochure. "We have quite a few commercials."

"What is it that you do?" Garza asked as he flipped through the brochure.

"My husband is an architect working with the city on restoration. San Pedro is our ground zero."

"You buy homes?" Garza asked.

"That's not all we do. We improve neighborhoods by increasing the values of older homes and work to improve the schools in the area."

"And Jorge sold his home to you? After twenty-five years?"

"I guess he felt like a change," Tina said with a chuckle.

Garza was silent.

"Would you care for some brownies?" Tina asked.

"Raises my blood sugar."

"Oh, you poor thing. I'll whip up a batch with some Splenda next time."

"Don't trouble yourself." Garza shut the door. He walked back to the garage where Lucy had managed to work her torso free of the suit. "Avon lady?" she asked.

"No. Tina Barnes."

"Who the hell is Tina Barnes?"

"Some broad with brownies—she gave me this."

Garza handed Lucy the brochure. Lucy frowned as she read.

"Fuckers," she said.

"What is it?"

"They want to improve your neighborhood."

"That's what she said—I think it means more cops."

"It means getting you out, so money comes in."

"They want my house?" Garza asked. He was growing agitated.

"You're five miles from the beach. Of course, they want your house. They want San Pedro to look like Santa Monica."

"But I hate the Westside."

"They think San Pedro is a shit-hole, but a shit-hole with potential," Lucy said as she struggled to completely free herself from the suit. "You mind helping me out of this thing? I'm about to piss myself."

Garza pulled the suit from Lucy's waist and she ran to the bathroom. He continued to read the brochure, paying close attention to the back page. There were five names and photos—each one a board member of the Phoenix Group. He went into the kitchen and placed the brochure in a drawer.

When Lucy returned, she was eager to spar with the dogs again. She put the suit back on. The suit consumed her, but it gave her confidence. She had beat Paco, lasted long enough for him to give up and release her. Lucy felt strong. Even when she thought Paco's teeth had pierced the suit and had found their way to her skin, she didn't let the fear beat her. She wondered if Garza had noticed—if he had been paying attention to the changes, she thought were so clear.

"You ready?" he asked, holding onto Sarge.

"Let him go," she said standing wide—her chest protruding forward.

The dog came charging, its awkward run made Lucy chuckle. Sarge's front legs were more dominant, strong and healthy, and surged forward—a reminder of what Sarge once was—while his hind legs trailed and worked to catch up. He was half a memory and half cold reality. She wondered what was going through his head. Did Sarge comprehend his malignancy? Did he see himself as broken? Maybe he had something to prove—maybe that's why he hit her so hard that she fell backwards and lost wind. He was upon her with fury. For a moment, Lucy thought about death. If he got her helmet off—got to her juggler, he could end her. She kept her chin down and her arms up. Sarge chewed the padding against her forearm, foamed at the mouth, growled. Lucy kept calm. She thought he'd gas out like Paco, but he didn't. He kept chewing at the helmet. She could smell his breath and felt heat. He wanted to kill her, and she wondered why. What was it about the suit that drew the dogs to her? What had Garza done to make the dogs see red?

Garza snatched Sarge back. He chained the dog and pulled Lucy out of the fray.

"Shit," she said, "what the hell!"

"He's got fight left in him."

"He was trying to kill me."

"What did you expect? Dog's probably got a dozen kills under his belt. It's how he's lasted this long."

Lucy removed her helmet. "And you think you can train him?"

"I know I can."

"Blood isn't it?" she asked.

"Say what?"

"The suit, you put blood on it."

"A little pig's blood in water."

"You could have told me."

"What's the fun in that?"

CHAPTER FIVE

THE DAYS CARRIED ON; the trainings more intense. The dogs learned various commands spoken mostly in Spanish. Garza had them on an all-natural diet: brown rice, peas, chicken and fish heads, all blended up and served in tin pans. He said he didn't trust what was in dog food, canned or dry. "If I wouldn't eat it, I damn sure wouldn't give it to them. Soldiers need good diets," he'd say.

Then the day came for the final test. Garza had woken early and was already dressed when he turned on the light and shook Lucy from her slumber.

"What?" she said, groggy and irritated from the brightness.

"Get up."

Lucy peeked from under the blanket. "It's still dark out."

Garza gave his signature glare.

"Okay. I'm up."

Lucy put on her clothes and met Garza outside. The dogs were awake. Garza had them chained on opposite ends of the yard.

"What was so important that you had to wake me at the butt-crack of dawn?" Lucy asked.

"It's time to see where we stand in the pack."

"The pack? That's what this is?"

"Of course."

"Do I need the suit for this?"

"No. This is the real thing. It's time to see where the dominance lies."

Garza walked over to Paco, got on all fours, and stared the dog in his eyes. The dog growled for a moment and then relented, producing a somber whine and dropping his head. Garza quickly rubbed between Paco's ears and the dog seemed to recover, panting and licking Garza's hand.

"What was that?" Lucy asked.

"I challenged him."

"It looked like you pissed him off."

"He understood his place. That's what matters"

"He could have chewed your face off."

"But he didn't because he understands the hierarchy."

"Fucking loco, man."

"Your turn."

"What?"

"You heard me," he said, "get on their level—test the bond."

"You may be some type of dog whisperer but I'm not. I don't need them to like me. I just need them to do what I say."

"What are you afraid of?"

"I don't know…getting mauled?"

"Respect is something that you haven't had much of in your life."

"Not this shit again. Look, I had a fucked-up life. Okay? Get over it. I have."

"You haven't! You got used to getting treated like shit. But with these dogs, either they respect you or they don't. But you've got to earn that kind of respect. I need to see that you've earned theirs'. You need to see it. Now get down."

Lucy began to approach Paco, and then got down on all fours. She crawled toward him and stopped about five inches from his snout. His eyes were fixed on her. He was tense in his shoulders. He bared his teeth, lunged, and swiped at her with his paw. Lucy jumped back. Sarge watched, unmoved, his paws were curled under his chest.

"Shit!"

"Relax," Garza said, "he's only looking to scare."

"So, this is a victory?"

"It's a start. But you're afraid and he knows it. Fear, chica, he smells it on you like a stink. And he'll call your bluff every time."

"Screw this. I'm going back to bed."

"No. We're going out."

"For what?"

"Supplies."

"Is anything opening now? The sun's not up."

"It will be by the time you get dressed. I'll scramble some eggs. Then we'll go."

"Just a heads up, I'm not much of a builder," Lucy said, "I've never even held a hammer."

"Who said we're building anything? Get dressed."

• • •

After breakfast, they drove the van north on Centre Street. It was still early, Lucy could have done with some caffeine but Garza brews it long, so it's strong and goes down like motor oil—she figured it would do more harm than good. Her stomach had been cramping all week; sharp pains. She feared an ulcer and tried her best not to think about it. She couldn't manage some ailment, not now. Like every woe in her life, she'd have to work through it.

Garza slowed the van as he approached a fenced in bungalow—brown stucco, iron bars over the windows. The home was the oldest on the block and soon would be the most modernized. Men were on the roof, ripping away what was left of it. A pile of shingles had collected next to a ladder. They were sawing off the iron bars, a reminder of a time when San Pedro was more dangerous, overrun with gangs— Crips, MS13s, and Neo Nazis. The town was too small to sustain them, as they were all operating blocks apart, south of Gaffey. When six-year-old Maritza Alvarez died, struck down in a drive-by, it was the last straw. LAPD came in heavy—they increased their patrols, instituted gang injunctions, and locked up every violent offender they could find. It was the dawning of a new day in San Pedro. And soon, white folks would be making their way back to the enclave by the beach; still cheap enough to live comfortably and have money left over for family trips to Disneyland. The *LA Times* called it *gentrification*—the opposite of 'white flight'. Garza now understood—it meant brown folks pushed further south, maybe into Long Beach or north, into Harbor City. He feared one-day San Pedro wouldn't have a brown face in sight. There would be overpriced real-estate, luxury high-rises overlooking the ports, yoga studios and trendy coffee shops, and the smells of sweet corn and chorizo— memories from an erased time.

Los Angeles didn't honor its past. It tore down its history and built glitz in its place—and it's always had a history of forgetting—a perpetual victim to the wrecking ball. Only the old-time Angelinos remembered the past—they were the purveyors of it—the 'good ole days' existed in stories told in barbershops, diners and bars. And through them, the city was remembered as more than sunshine, palms and movie stars, but for what it was—a second chance for those fleeing Europe, soldiers looking for new beginnings after the war, Blacks escaping the racism in the South and Mexicans escaping the violence in Mexico. The city embodied possibilities, and it was the shimmering cathedral for dreamers, gangsters, and everything in between.

"Whose house is that?" Lucy asked.

"Tina Barnes."

"The chick in the jogging suit?"

"Yes."

"You got a thing for her or something?"

"That was my friend Jorge's house."

"I didn't think you had any friends."

"He said he would never sell."

"I guess he changed his mind. They must have offered him *mucho dinero.*"

"A person's word should mean something."

"Maybe he just needed the cash? People get hard up you know—they fall on hard times. Or she made him an offer he couldn't refuse? I mean money moves mountains."

"Some things should matter more than money."

Lucy laughed. "You have been in that house too long. Nothing's more important than money. Isn't that why you're helping me?"

Garza knew it was more than money that made him decide to help Lucy, but it wasn't worth bringing up. It was something only he understood. And tonight, he would reclaim the past and get back a piece of what he had lost—all in the name of Gazpacho.

He gassed the van, pumped the clutch and shifted. The transmission jerked hard and the van pushed forward, easing through stop signs until it reached Gaffey. It squealed to a stop, and then made a right turn, eastbound.

The hardware store was a small 'mom and pop' operation, established in San Pedro around 1952; it had seen generations of family ownership. Inside, a young man behind the counter knew Garza by the name Hector. Lucy didn't inquire why, she didn't have to. In her research, she had learned Garza cultivated many aliases over the years, and figured Hector was just one of them.

Garza knew where everything in the store was located and moved efficiently down the aisles, picking up plywood and long nails. Before leaving, Garza asked the young man about his grandmother: "How's your abuelita?"

"Still in the hospital," the young man said, "but she got your flowers."

"Good."

"Is this your granddaughter?" the young man asked.

Lucy was quiet, unsure of what to say and curious of Garza's response.

"Yes," Garza answered, "this is Lucita."

Lucy shook the young man's hand.

"It's rare nowadays…teenagers hanging with their grandparents. It's nice to see," the young man said.

The idea of being someone's grandkid made Lucy smile, but the aged killer's lie was the closest she'd ever get to being someone's granddaughter. Garza hurried out of the hardware store, and Lucy followed behind. Garza loaded the plywood into the back of the van. Lucy stood watching him.

"What was that back there?" she asked, "that line about me being your granddaughter."

"An old man with a young girl at his side ain't right, unless they're related."

"Does anyone know you? The real you, I mean."

"A retired cop was coming around for a few years. He'd park outside the house and watch the front. Then he stopped showing up—he probably died. The old sack was huge. He needed a cane just to stand upright. Nobody outside of him probably know who I am. Most people think I'm dead."

"But you knew that guy's grandmother. Who do they think you are?"

"A retired longshoreman."

"Maybe you should visit her?"

"Mind your own business."

"Just saying…maybe you wouldn't be so lonely."

"Who the hell says I'm lonely? Worry about yourself."

"Okay. Shit. Sorry I brought it up."

Garza had lived lies for so long that they had become truth. Every relationship seemed built upon falsehood—it was a kind of prison, having to keep a lie fed after giving birth to it so long ago; the lie existing throughout generations, changing over time and becoming cemented. What had Garza done for the woman in the hospital? And if she knew who he really was, would it change how she saw him? Can any good deed outweigh a lifetime of wrong?

• • •

In a few hours, night would fall. They didn't have much time to prepare. Garza had fashioned a workshop in the garage—a place to prep for the killing. He filled a spray bottle with watered-down pig's blood and laid out four pieces of plywood. In a duffle bag, he put in a hammer, work gloves, and ski masks.

The dogs were irritated. He could hear them growl and whine. They were likely hungry, and, in a few hours, they would feed. He put his dog whistle in his pocket. The dogs had learned his commands, but he understood that in the grip of frenzy, they could be difficult to call back. The whistle assured their quick return.

Lucy came into the garage. She was dressed in a black long-sleeved shirt and pants. Her hair was pulled into a ponytail.

"What if they see us?" she asked.

"They'll be asleep. Probably passed out."

"How do you know?"

"Because I've been clocking them—watching the comings and goings for some time. Two of them have jobs and leave the house around 7:30 in the morning. The other one sleeps until noon, orders pizza and gets drunk on the porch until 3:00, that's when the other two typically arrive."

"How long have you been watching them?"

"A long time."

"Before they took your dog, you mean?"

"Yes."

"They've been bothering you that long?"

"I guess so."

"So why not do something about them earlier? Why tonight?"

"Because tonight I've got you."

Lucy smiled. It made her feel good to be a part of something and that Garza needed her.

"Then tonight should feel good," she said.

"It will."

They drove to the boys' home and parked the van around the corner. They sat for a moment as the dogs stirred in the back of the van.

"It's quiet tonight," Lucy said.

"Let's keep it that way. We'll move through the alleyway— it should be clear," Garza said.

Garza took two pieces of plywood from the van and

walked down the alley to the boy's house. As quiet as he could, he nailed the wood across the boys' front door. Lucy went back to the van to check on the dogs, who were gnawing on dried pig ears. They had already gone a full day without food and were growing more aggressive. Garza moved onto to the backdoor; he nailed wood across the door posts and returned to the van. Lucy brought the dogs from the van and walked them toward a window adjacent to the living room. Garza sprayed the pig's blood around the window. The dogs jumped up against the house; their paws braced against its side. They licked at the pig's blood. Lucy pushed up on the window to find it unlocked. She wasn't surprised, after all she figured the boys were usually drunk or high and likely didn't bother checking such things. She pushed the window up for the dogs. Garza spoke a command in Spanish and the dogs leaped into the house.

The moon was bright, and the streets remained empty. Lucy and Garza returned to the van and waited.

"How long do you think this will take?" she asked.

"Not much longer," Garza said holding a gold stopwatch.

"What if someone calls the police?"

"In this neighborhood?"

"It's so quiet. What if they didn't carry out the command? They could be pissing on the living room floor for all we know."

"Relax."

"I'm going to see if I can hear anything."

Lucy got out of the van and began walking toward the house.

"Where the hell are you going?" Garza asked.

Lucy began to walk faster. Garza got out of the van and rushed after her.

"Slow down, damn-it," he said.

"The dogs could be hurt."

"Just wait."

Garza took the dog whistle from his pocket and gave three blows.

"I said stop." Garza grabbed Lucy's arm. She faced him abruptly.

"Don't take another step," he said.

Lucy didn't move. The dogs appeared from around the boys' house. Their chops were stained with blood—their paws coated in it. Garza blew the whistle again and the dogs picked up speed—a full gallop, tongues flailing about. He quickly placed leashes around their necks and led them back to the van. He opened the van door to let the dogs in.

Inside, he fed them pig ears and they began to calm down. Lucy huddled in the passenger seat as Garza started the engine. She didn't speak a word. He circled the block twice before pulling into his garage. In the garage, he washed the blood from the dogs with a garden hose.

"We're fucked," Lucy said, "you left the plywood on the door and everything."

"Were you in that house?" he asked.

"No."

"Then don't worry about it."

"How can you be so calm?"

"Because when it comes to evidence, there won't be any."

"What if someone survived?"

"Then it's on your head. You had me call them back early, so you better hope they finished the job."

"What do we do now?"

"Nothing."

"And the police?" she asked, "what happens when they show up?"

"They'll walk the neighborhood and ask questions."

"And the dogs?"

"We ain't the only pet owners on the block."

"What about DNA?"

"From the dogs?"

"It could happen—like *CSI* shit."

"Think about the crime scene—how truly fucked up it is. It's an animal attack? The amount of effort it will take to solve what happened to those pieces of shit isn't going to be worth the man hours. They are victims without value. Chances are the cops are going to find drugs and guns in that house. Maybe even enough to suggest they were selling. If they were felons or bangers, we have even less to worry about."

Garza went into his bedroom and shut the door. Lucy sat on the sofa. She was sure at any moment sirens would sound, but the sirens never came. All night, she tried to sleep, to quiet her thoughts enough for an hour or two, but she couldn't. The boys were likely dead, the dogs had done what they were trained to do, and in a few days their decomposing bodies would inform the neighborhood of their demise.

Life in Garza's house carried on. Over the following weeks, Garza continued to train the dogs—introducing new commands and killing techniques. They became more savage, and he was pleased. He started feeding them the best cuts of meat—said they had earned it. Garza had changed, something had awakened inside of him. He was vital and alert in a way Lucy hadn't seen before.

It was a Saturday when the odor of the boys' bodies kicked up enough stink in the neighborhood for the police to be called. When the police arrived, they entered the house and came out quickly. Some officers were vomiting on the lawn, others simply paced as if they were trying to get a handle on the scene. Lucy watched from a window as they carried the bodies out in sealed bags and loaded them into a coroner's van.

"Now what?" Lucy asked Garza, who was watching TV.

"Let them do what they do."

"They've got the plywood. It's in bags. They're taking a lot of pictures."

"It's their jobs. Besides, almost half of the homicides in L.A. go unsolved. The cops have bigger cases than a few torn up gangbangers."

Lucy kept watch until the coroner van left. Detectives began to canvas the neighborhood. Garza continued to watch the Dodger game.

The doorbell rang. Garza looked to Lucy: "You better answer it," he said.

Lucy cautiously went to the door. When she opened it, a gruff man in a brown sport coat stood holding a notepad and pen. He flashed his badge.

"Hello," she said.

"Hello miss. I'm Detective McMichael with the LAPD. Can I ask you some questions?"

"About what?"

"We're investigating the deaths of your neighbors. They resided in the home just off the alley. We want to know if you heard anything."

"Well, shit. Is that what I was smelling?"

"Most likely."

"Did you know them?"

"No. What happened?"

"That's what we're trying to figure out. What type of neighbors they were?"

"What do you mean?"

"Were they friendly, civil?"

"They were drunks who smoked weed and played loud music."

"You ever speak to them? Or interact?"

"No."

"But you know they smoked weed and drank?" McMichael asked.

"I could smell it and I saw them on the porch...drinking."

"You know if anyone in the neighborhood ever had an altercation with them?"

"I keep to myself," she said tapping her foot against the carpet.

"You live here alone?"

"My grandfather stays here but he's ill."

"Baseball fan?"

"What?"

"You got the game on," McMichael said.

"I need to get back to my grandfather."

The detective scribbled some notes. "Of course. I appreciate your time," he said. McMichael reached into his suit pocket and pulled out a business card. "Here. In case you think of something."

Lucy took the card and shut the door. She returned to the window to watch as the detective conversed with his partner, a black woman dressed in a pair of creased slacks and a cream blouse. They watched the house for a moment and then walked down the alley.

Garza had slipped into the kitchen when Lucy answered the door. He reappeared with a beer in hand.

"You did well," he said. "I don't see them hanging around for very long."

"Confident much?"

"When things settle, we'll move forward with the plan."

Garza finished the beer and disposed of the empty can in the garbage. Lucy removed it and set it on the counter.

"What now?" he asked.

"It's called recycling."

Garza sighed and returned to the sofa to finish the baseball game.

The detectives came around again the following week and requested everyone with a dog to provide their phone number, birthdate and full name. Garza's home was registered under one of his aliases. Lucy gave the false information to the female detective. She seemed satisfied.

Over the following weeks, rumors spread throughout the neighborhood that the boys had gotten high and attacked each other. There was little mention of the plywood since the police weren't sharing the details in the case. The consensus was the boys were a blight in the neighborhood and wouldn't be missed.

The house was later boarded up by the city. 'Keep Out' and 'No Trespassing' signs were posted, though they didn't stop the kids a few blocks over from trying to break in. Everyone wanted to see the slaughterhouse.

● ● ●

It was early morning when Garza met Lucy in the kitchen. He had already made coffee, toast, scrambled eggs and bacon. Lucy took a seat at the table.

"The cops won't be back," he said, "time to finish what we started."

"Okay."

"Shit—I haven't considered who the target is. So, who's the *sancho*?"

Lucy hesitated.

"Don't tell me you're getting cold feet. Killing those little bastards was a practice run."

"I know."

"You scared?"

"No."

"Don't lie to me," Garza said, "you better be scared."

"I am scared but that's not it. It's the target. It's more complicated than I let on."

Garza looked puzzled. "Complicated?"

"Give me the name."

"It's Victor. Victor Soto."

"Name sounds familiar. Why do I know that name?"

"Everyone in Los Angeles knows that name. He's an assistant district attorney."

"Bullshit!"

"He wasn't Assistant D.A. when he killed my mother," Lucy said.

"You didn't think it was worth a mention before? Maybe when you first showed up on my doorstep with your little sob story?"

"I knew you'd turn me down."

"Damn right."

"I don't care who he is now. It doesn't erase what he's done."

"What he's done," Garza said snidely.

"My mother didn't deserve…"

"Your mother was a junkie."

"What did you say?" Tears began to well Lucy's eyes.

"Easy girl, easy."

"You're a real son-of-a-bitch."

"Come with me," he said.

Lucy followed Garza into his room where he opened a closet. Inside, stacks of newspaper clippings occupied the space. Some dating back thirty years. "I may not get out much, but I know what's going on. I keep up on this city and all the dirt, especially anybody and everybody who dies— Jane and John Doe's, celebrities, politicians—everybody."

"It's a museum of death," Lucy said somewhat disgusted.

"Thank you."

Garza removed a trimmed article from a grocery bag filled with various clippings that had aged brown and yellow.

"Took a while to register in my head but I remembered her name from this article," Garza said.

Garza handed Lucy the paper clipping.

"Her body washed up around Venice Pier. Cops thought she got high, slipped, maybe hit her head a few times on the rocks and died there," Garza said.

The color from Lucy's face drained. "It wasn't an accident. That night she called me. She said she was at some party and she'd be home in a few hours. I waited and waited, but she never came. When I called back, a man answered her phone. He was hysterical—crying. I couldn't understand him. I asked where my mother was and then he hung up. They found her the next morning."

"And you know for certain that it's Soto?" Garza asked.

"One day I hear the voice again in a campaign commercial. I recognized it right away and I've followed that voice ever since. Every election, every speech. Waiting until I could silence it forever."

"So why the talk of dope?" Garza asked.

"My mom had a problem, sure, but she was turning things around. She had gotten out of treatment a month before she died. She promised she wouldn't use again. She was pretty, and men liked her. She thought dating would do her some good and wanted to meet a nice man."

"Sometimes people break promises no matter how hard they try to keep them."

"You speak from experience?"

"No. I never make promises. Too much of a burden."

"My mother had her flaws—she didn't deserve to die. Soto is out there going on with his life—living it up. He's got money, a career, the nice house, a family…"

"And it's not fair," Garza said mockingly.

"I understand if you want to back out."

"I've killed important men before."

Garza went to the kitchen and took Tina Barnes's brochure from the drawer. He handed the brochure to Lucy.

"Read the names on the back," he said.

"Victor Soto?"

"He's a partner in the Phoenix Group."

Lucy took her smart phone from her pocket and browsed the internet for the Phoenix Group.

"Soto is more than that—he's a key investor. Along with a Taylor Barnes, probably Tina's husband."

"It's going to take more planning."

"So, what's the move?"

"He has children and a wife, right?"

"A son," Lucy said, "his wife died years ago. His son works in Marina Del Rey. At a rest home."

"He's a nurse?"

"Something like that."

Garza laughs. "A male nurse? It is a new day."

"Men aren't just doctors, you know? Might do you some good to get out occasionally," Lucy said.

"You should take a few days. Sleep in your own bed— relax. I need time to think."

"All right."

Later, Lucy packed a few things, fed the dogs and caught the bus on Gaffey and 9th. It felt strange leaving Garza alone in the house. She had grown accustomed to being there and though she knew he would never admit it, Garza had grown fond of her as well.

CHAPTER SIX

LUCY OPENED THE DOOR and entered her apartment—it felt foreign. The room stunk of garbage. She had forgotten to dump the trash. She bagged up the garbage and set it outside the door. She had left dishes in the sink—food crusted on cheap China. She ran hot water over the plates and glasses and chipped at the hard debris with the tip of a knife.

After cleaning her apartment, she logged onto her laptop and opened the file containing all things Victor Soto—for Lucy, reviewing the collected data was like taking a vitamin supplement, it made her feel good and helped keep her focused on her mission. It stoked her fire, that merciless need to see him dead. She knew everything there was to know about the city's illustrious Assistant D.A. She had learned about his rise to city council and then his appointment to Assistant District Attorney. The company he kept—politicians, activists, and the Hollywood and Silicon Valley types. She had uncovered his school records from his time at Stanford. During his senior year, a woman had alleged sexual battery—citing the "grabbing of her breasts and buttocks." The charges were dropped.

The woman did not return the following semester. Prior to his election to the city council, the *LA Weekly* ran an expose and deemed him the victim of a misunderstanding and questioned the credibility of the female co-ed—something about drugs, alcohol, and her predilection for the company of wealthy male students. From that day on, the media loved Victor Soto and never printed one moot word about him.

His son, Martin Soto, was listed as staff on the website of a convalescent home in Marina Del Rey—palatial grounds fashioned like a quaint resort. A photo on the home's website showed him dressed in tacky Hawaiian print scrubs standing in front of palm trees. Martin's face wasn't like his father's. It was boyish and without pretense. He looked charming while his father embodied deception—creased brow, the bleached veneered smile, pudginess held together in an expensive suit.

Victor's wife had passed from cancer years before. She was referenced in a few newspaper articles online and by all accounts, she was a lovely woman. She had a charity organization that provided support to families afflicted by cancer. She formed the 501c when she received her diagnosis— colon cancer. Prior to that, she worked in finance. Since her passing, Lucy wondered what Victor and his son's relationship had been reduced to. Did the death of wife and mother bring them closer, or had it relegated them to adversaries? Two men trying to make sense of why the most important woman in their lives was taken so young, and the angst that comes with watching her die. But Lucy had no sympathy for them—at least they got to say goodbye.

Lucy ordered Chinese—steamed vegetables and rice. It was a break from Garza's cooking, but she missed being there with the dogs. Downtown was louder than San Pedro—Lucy got minimal rest and woke tired. She made toast and had a grapefruit for breakfast. Afterwards, she got dressed and took the bus to Marina Del Rey. An idea had come to her in the night as she laid in bed, restless. She could put on a rouse at the convalescent home where Soto's son worked; she'd pretend to be Garza's granddaughter—it had worked before at the hardware store and with the police, and now she'd wear the mask again. But rather than deflect investigators, she'd play the role of concerned granddaughter looking to put Garza in a home where he could be looked after. She could get close to the son, friend him on social media and maybe get insight into his family. She hoped it would lead to learning more about Victor Soto. It was worth a shot. After all, friending someone on social media was Lucy's generation's version of a handshake. Lucy knew it wouldn't be easy; outside of Garza and Kip, she didn't have much experience holding a conversation for long, especially not with an 'everyday' person. It gave her anxiety to think she'd have to talk to a stranger about absolutely nothing of substance— but it was a necessary burden.

The bus dropped her off on Lincoln Boulevard, a few miles south of Loyola Marymount University. It was a school she once dreamt of attending. She had toured the campus in high school as part of a college preparatory field trip. Lucy knew early in school that college wouldn't be attainable, but it didn't hurt to dream. Aside from the cost, her social ineptitude would have made it impossible for her to make friends. But despite not having a formal education, she managed to survive. She learned all she could about computers and honed her ability to research; then, she marketed herself as a cyber-investigator and computer tech. She was a half-decent hacker, too, and for the right price she could steal photos and files from most smartphones and laptops, but in the last five years, she had distanced herself from backdoor hacking and scouring the dark web. She was totally legitimate; most of her clients were private detectives who didn't have time or the know-how to research on the internet. They gave her the search parameters and she delivered in a day or two—she was trustworthy and came highly recommended, even though no one had ever seen her face. The assignments paid well, and she could work from home in her pajamas.

Lucy walked a block until she arrived at Sunset Crest Assisted Living—it was nicer than any apartment complex she had ever lived. As she entered, a jovial man with a recessed hairline approached.

"Greetings. I'm Brad. Do you have an appointment?"

"No, I don't. I'm looking at facilities for my grandfather. Your reviews were pretty good."

"That they are," he said, "in fact, we've won quite a few awards over the years, as you can see."

Brad pointed to framed plaques on the wall in the entry way. "How about I show you around?"

Lucy smiled. "Sure."

"And what was your name?"

"Lucy."

"Right this way, Lucy."

Lucy followed behind Brad—a pudgy man in a teal polo shirt and khakis. The facility's logo—the sun rising over a mountain range was stitched on his right chest pocket. He led Lucy through French doors and into a courtyard where people sat talking, playing board games, and drinking iced tea.

"As you can see, our residents are very content. We try our best to cater to each of their needs. May I ask what your grandfather's condition is?"

Lucy paused for a moment. "He forgets things."

"Dementia or Alzheimer's?"

"Dementia. He's still not ready to accept that he's not as

sharp as he once was."

"We see our fair share of that. And does he take medications?"

"No."

"He must be in the early stages? If he ever needs medication of any kind, we can administer it here. We're a one-stop shop."

"How many do you have on staff?"

"It's a total of thirteen staff members on around-the-clock rotations."

The facility was impressive, and Lucy wondered if Garza would be happier in a place like Sunset Crest, rather than rotting away in a dilapidated house in San Pedro. But the thought was short-lived; she knew Garza wouldn't last a day in a place like that.

"Speaking of staff, here is Marty. He's one of our nursing assistants."

Martin was fit and had a deep tan. He likely spent his free time surfing and running on the beach. Unlike Brad, whose polo was tucked neatly into his khakis, Martin's polo hung loosely at his waist. He smiled and extended his hand for Lucy to shake.

"Martin."

"Lucy."

"Brad is giving you the tour, I see. Have you had a chance to see our game room?"

"No, we just started."

"It's pretty great. We have memory games all designed to help maintain and improve cognitive function."

"That's right," Brad said, "it is Marty's pride and joy. He worked very hard on getting that little room together."

Martin cut his eyes at Brad. "I'm a psych major—it's nice to put what I learn into practice. I've got a few minutes before I go on break. I can take over the tour…if you don't mind, Brad?"

"Not at all, Marty. There are always things to tend to in the office. It was a pleasure meeting you, Lucy." Brad handed her his card. "Let me know if I can be of assistance."

"Thank you, Brad."

Brad headed back toward the main office. When he was out of sight, Martin let out a sigh of relief. "The guy means well but he can be a little much."

"You think?" Lucy said.

"I was trying to be delicate—guy's a real tool."

"Then I guess you saved me from the lamest tour ever."

"So, who are you looking to place here?"

"My grandfather."

"You're his caretaker?"

"Yes."

"Not too many people our age doing that these days. You two close?"

"We've grown closer in the last few months since he's gotten sick."

"Sickness has a way of bringing people closer. It's nice you're looking out for him," Martin said. "How about checking out the game room?"

"Lead the way."

● ● ●

After the tour, Martin walked Lucy outside. They stood in front of the building as the traffic flowed down Lincoln. The sun hadn't yet burned away the fog—there was moisture in the air.

"I hope it works out for your grandfather here," Martin said.

"It might be a hard sell. He can be a little stubborn."

"Sounds like my dad. They don't always know what's best for them."

"Are you two close?"

"We used to be closer. He works a lot and sometimes we don't see much of each other."

Lucy felt nervous and didn't know what to say. She wanted to know more about his father but being too aggressive with questioning could spook him.

She put her hands into her pockets and shrugged. "I should probably get going. Thanks for the tour."

"It was my pleasure, Lucy."

Lucy smiled and began to walk toward the bus stop, when Martin called to her: "You a Ramones fan?"

Lucy looked back. "Yeah, of course."

"There's a decent cover band playing tonight in Alhambra. You interested?"

"Maybe." Lucy felt a tinge of anxiety and moistness form in her arm pits. "What time?" she asked in a soft voice.

"They get going around ten o' clock."

"It's been a while since I've been to a show."

"You want my number in case you're up for it?" Martin asked.

"You're number?"

"Yeah—that weird?"

"No, I just thought everyone DM'd these days."

"Guess I'm old school."

"All right."

Lucy saved Martin's number in her cell phone.

"I better get back," she said.

"Okay."

"Hope to see you later."

"Cool."

● ● ●

She took the bus back to Garza's house. When she arrived, he was hesitant to let her in—repeatedly asking, "Who's there? What the hell do you want?"

After realizing it was Lucy, he opened the door. He was haggard and looked hungover.

"You smell horrible," she said.

He stumbled to the sofa.

"Damn. You're drunk off your ass," she said.

"I needed some time to myself."

"Yeah, clearly. Have the dogs eaten?"

"I fed them a few hours ago."

"Okay."

Lucy took a seat next to Garza on the sofa. "I met Soto's son, Martin."

"That right?"

"Yes, and I have a plan. Well, part of a plan."

"Let's hear it."

"I want to check you into a convalescent home. It's where Martin works."

Garza laughed. "To hell with that."

"Hear me out. We check you into the home where he works. It'll give me a reason to hang around there. I milk him for more information about his dad."

"Then what? I snatch the kid?" Garza smiles.

"No. We aren't hurting Martin."

"Why not? Did it to a guy in Lawndale once. He owed a whole lot of money. We held his brother for three days. Then we sent him home missing all his fingers and toes. We nailed a note to his chest with an address—told the guy his wife was next unless he showed up. Like clockwork, guy shows up and the dogs got fed."

"So, he didn't have the money to pay back?"

"I don't know. Probably not."

"You didn't give him the chance to pay off his debt?"

"It wasn't about the money no more. It was about the principle. He failed to deliver on what was agreed—simple as that. A man looks you in the eye. He shakes and blows. You take him at his word. The moment his word goes to shit—he becomes less than shit, like a dirt speck."

"I'm not sure I want to involve him, okay?"

"Are you going soft on me? Don't forget what I told you. Leverage comes in many forms. If that means I take his son's ear to get his attention, I do it."

"Fine. Whatever. I'm seeing him tonight."

"The kid?"

"Yes."

"What for?"

"To get him on the hook. I'll ask him more about his dad. Figure out where Soto likes to spend his time and when he'll be isolated."

Garza glared. "Sounds risky. Keep your head on straight."

"You don't have to worry about me. Come this time next week, Victor Soto will be down in the ground."

"The sooner the better."

"You tired of me already?"

"You're messy."

"Are you kidding me? Look at this place. There's at least two inches of dust on everything."

Garza grunted. "What time you going to be home?"

"Not sure. You got a spare key? That way I won't wake you."

"I think I do somewhere, but I don't like giving people keys to my shit."

"Don't be so paranoid. You really think I'd try to rip you off?"

"Nobody would be that fucking stupid."

"Exactly."

"So?"

"Yeah," he said, "I'll get you a key."

CHAPTER SEVEN

LUCY TOOK TWO BUSES getting to Alhambra. The concert was held in an old warehouse. They were giving away beer and cheap wine at the door. Martin was waiting near the stage in a black shirt, jeans and boots. He was toying with his phone and sipping a beer. When Lucy saw him, she regretted not freshening up before she left—she smelled of Garza's house, cigarettes and the dogs.

"Hey," she said.

Martin looked up and smiled. "You made it."

"I did."

"Awesome. I was about to text you."

A short blonde girl approached Martin. She had a clipboard in hand and a walkie-talkie attached to her hip. "The band is here."

"Great," Martin said looking at his watch. "Only ten minutes late. Have them start setting up."

"Wait. Is this like your thing? Are you a promoter or something?" Lucy asked.

"Not exactly. I put on shows for a nonprofit—an

organization my mom started. We raise money for cancer research."

"That's cool."

"It's doing some good. I put on the showcase every year. This year some of the money is going to my dad's organization as well."

"Your dad's organization?"

"It's a city revitalization project called Phoenix."

"Revitalization?" she asked.

"You know? Like taking low-income parts of town and building them up. Most of it is enticing businesses to set up shop and hire locally. Right now, he has South Central and San Pedro in his crosshairs."

"Really? What's great about Pedro?"

"He says it's prime—beach access, homes with views of Catalina, decent school system. Only problem is getting there."

"The buses run."

"That's what I said. Of course, he thinks he can do better—he's talking about putting in a rail line that runs right down the Harbor Freeway with a depot on Gaffey."

"Has your dad always been wanting to *improve* the city?"

"Not always. But after my mom passed, he changed. He started doing more humanitarian work and using his position as A.D.A. to do more than look out for his rich pals. It's like he became a new man."

"What was he like before?"

Martin took another sip from his beer and wiped the residue from his lips with the back of his hand. "Let's say you wouldn't want to be stuck at a dinner table with him. My dad has a way of rubbing people wrong sometimes. For a while we lived more like roommates instead of father and son."

"Strong personality?"

"That's one way of putting it?"

"Is there another way?" Lucy snickered.

"Yeah—a dick. I'm going to get another beer. You want one?"

"Sure," Lucy said.

Martin returned with two cans. "They're already out of bottles," he said as he handed Lucy beer.

"What is it you do, exactly? I mean when you're not looking after your grandfather."

Lucy shrugged. "Not too much. I work from home and kind of keep to myself."

"What's your line of work?"

"Investigations."

"Like a P.I.?"

"More like a researcher. I find information on people—search databases, criminal records—the sort of thing a lot of investigators don't have time for."

"I can't say I've met a sleuth before."

"Trust me. It's not as cool as it sounds."

"Does it leave time for a social life?"

"Not really. This is the first time I've been out in years."

"You serious?"

"I am."

"You don't date? Not that anything is wrong with that," he said.

"I tend to keep things casual. You?"

"It's been a while. I don't meet many potential girlfriends where I work."

"The geriatric crowd just doesn't do it for you, huh?"

Martin laughed. "You want to meet the band?"

"Why not?"

Lucy followed Martin toward the rear of the stage. The warehouse was filled with people—they cut through the crowd until they reached a door. They entered to find the band tuning their instruments and drinking beer. Martin introduced them to an unimpressed Lucy. They all sat a while talking music; Martin and Lucy stayed in the room after the band had gone out to play. Martin was a wealth of knowledge about the Los Angeles punk scene. Under different circumstances, Lucy would have been more engaged and less guarded. But Garza's voice was doing laps in her head— she couldn't forget the mission. Martin was just a mark, a means to an end. When she felt his interest slipping or if he was gauging if she was bored, she'd ask a question and send him on another tangent.

They returned to watch the band for the last set. Lucy had another beer and Martin refrained, telling her he needed all his faculties for the ride home.

"You ever been on a bike?" he asked.

"Is this when you ask if I need a ride home?"

"Maybe."

"It would beat taking the bus."

"A bus at this hour? Could be dangerous."

"I handle myself pretty well."

"I don't doubt that."

Lucy paused for a moment. "Well, you know San Pedro?"

"That's where you live?"

"Yes."

"Outside of my dad's projects I don't know much about it," he said, "I've never even been to one of his work sites. What freeway do we take?"

"Harbor South—it's a straight shot. It runs you right into Pedro."

"Sounds easy enough."

"You got an extra helmet?" Lucy asked.

"I got you covered."

"I'm not going to call you Maverick or anything," she said.

Martin laughed. "Give me a second to tell the guys we're heading out. They can take care of the cleanup."

● ● ●

The motorcycle ripped loudly in the night. Lucy gripped the rear of the bike—it was red, light weight—an Asian make. Before getting on, Martin had given her one instruction. "Go with the lean. Don't fight it," he said, "otherwise we might lose our balance."

She felt free and liked the way the air curled and wrapped around her body—they traveled down the center lane. The freeway was almost empty. The bike sped past cars speckled in lanes; Lucy knew the cars were moving but they might have well been still as the motorcycle flew past them. Lucy tightened her arms around his waist. She liked the feeling— her chest pressed against his back—her T-shirt against the thickness of his leather jacket. Perhaps she was truly cured of her anxiety? The first dose of medicine being Garza and now it was Martin racing down the 110; the final injection that made her heart pound and sweat bead behind her ears. Her anxiety replaced with a need for adrenalin. As the bike reached 80 miles per hour, she no longer considered the danger; instead, she demanded for more speed.

She shouted: "Faster, Martin. Faster!"

He gradually increased the bike's speed, reaching 90 miles per hour before slowing down as they drove under the arching bridge above the freeway. The bridge doubled as a welcome sign. The words, "San Pedro", were lit in blue neon. The taggers hadn't defaced the letters, even they displayed an ounce of pride for the blue-collared marine town. Martin down-shifted the bike to a soft rumble, as he came to a stop at the red light.

"You can let me off at Twelfth Street," Lucy said.

Martin nodded. The cross streets were numbered sequentially. When the light turned green, he cruised forward. He made a right on Twelfth Street and stopped the bike on the corner of Pacific. He removed his helmet and Lucy climbed off the bike.

"Drop you here?" he asked. "It's the middle of nowhere."

"I stay down there," Lucy said, pointing down a dark street.

"I can take you the whole way. It's no problem. Unless..."

"Unless what?" she asked.

"Unless you don't want me to know where you live?"

"We did just meet."

"I'm not a creeper," Martin said.

"Well that's a confession."

"The only thing worthy of confessing is that I'm about as lame as they come."

"I kind of figured that with all the music history talk."

"Since when is music history lame?" Martin asked as he popped out the kickstand and got off the bike.

"It's not but most guys wouldn't have wasted time schooling me. They would have shared enough to impress me and then made their play to get into my pants. Unless..."

"Unless what?"

"Your version of sweet talk is seducing me with dates, facts and humming *God Save The Queen*."

"I'm afraid I'm not that smooth."

"Or maybe you're out of practice?"

Martin took Lucy by the hand and pulled her close; she didn't resist. He kissed her and cupped the side of her face with his hand. He embraced her until they both felt the need to gasp for air. As he pulled away, Lucy's eyes were still closed. When she opened them, moisture had formed.

"Shit. I'm sorry. I shouldn't have done that," he said.

"No. It was nice, Martin—it's been a long time since I've wanted to be kissed by someone." Lucy wiped the moisture from her eyes.

"Okay," Martin said, "I smelled the ocean on the ride in. How close are we?"

"I'm pretty sure the beach is closed."

"It's a clear night—be a shame to let it go to waste."

"Don't tell me you're into stargazing," Lucy said.

"What if I am?"

"Do you write sonnets, too?"

"Come on."

"All right, Romeo. Just for a little while."

"Deal."

"I know a place," Lucy said as she climbed back on the bike. Martin started the engine and continued down Gaffey Street. After a few turns, at Lucy's direction, he parked at a look-out, near an iron fence, where the ocean breeze gently blew. There was a cliff-face above, and the rocky shore was a few feet away.

"What is this place?" he asked.

"You'll see," Lucy said.

Lucy used the light of her cellphone to guide her. She approached a hole that had been cut into the fence. "I think we have to go in this way," she said.

Martin hesitated, looking to a no trespassing sign that stated violators would be prosecuted. Lucy scoffed. "You're really worried about that? C'mon."

Lucy slipped her body through the hole. Martin followed. They made their way up a path of stone slabs and concrete. Martin was careful of his footing—the terrain was unpredictable—mud holes and concrete shards. When he'd stumble, Lucy would extend her hand for him to take hold and regain his balance. Once they reached the trail's peak, Lucy stood gazing out at the ocean.

"This view is definitely worth the effort," Martin said. "How did you find this place?"

"The internet. I always wanted to see it. I never had much reason to come out here until my grandfather got sick."

They were surrounded by ruins. Concrete blocks were all that was left of walls that once shaped bungalows. Graffiti gave color to the dusted industrial landscape. The only things growing were three palm trees that perhaps had survived the decades old catastrophe that sent the town's edge into the ocean.

"They call it Sunken City," Lucy said.

"Not the most original name. What caused it to sink?"

"Not sure. Bad luck?"

"You think people died here?"

"No. The city evacuated the residents and even had their homes moved. Well, most of the homes."

"So, you also have a thing for L.A. history? I was thinking I was boring you earlier tonight."

"No, you weren't."

"I never get used to this," Martin said.

"Used to what?" Lucy asked.

"The ocean."

Lucy smiled.

"If I had my way, I'd surf all-day. Maybe even live on a boat just so I could take trips to Catalina whenever I felt like it."

"Sounds like a sweet life."

"Could get lonely, though," Martin said, "there's always room for a first mate."

"You mean like your assistant?"

"More like a co-captain. If you're interested?"

Lucy sighed. "I don't even know what I'm doing here."

"We're enjoying the view."

"That's not what I mean."

"I was joking about the co-captain thing," he said. "I'm not even sure why I said that? I don't think a woman's place is as a co-captain or anything."

"You ever wonder if this was all a mistake?"

"What? Like us hanging out?"

"No—I mean life. This ocean, these rocks—being on this planet floating in space. I mean terrible things happen to us, here. We do terrible things to each other. We suffer. We lose people. They're taken from us. It's hell and we're just supposed to keep going? It's a trap, really. I mean eighty years of suffering if you're lucky and then you just cease to be?"

"It depends how you chose to live your life, I guess. But I don't think life is an accident, Lucy. It can have purpose—it can have meaning."

"You make it sound like we're in control. We don't control shit, Martin. We react, we change, we try to adapt—that's it."

"I guess I'm too much of a romantic to believe that," Martin said, "There's beauty even in the ugliness."

Lucy looked at Martin—he was brimming with hope and possibility. Lucy knew she was dealt shitty cards in life, but Martin had a few aces. Maybe that's why he couldn't see it—the shear pain of it all. She wanted desperately to believe as he did, but the only purpose she had in life was to kill his father and she knew she was failing at that.

"It's pretty late. We should head back," Lucy said.

Lucy headed down the trail and Martin followed. She was quiet and distant. Martin struggled to find the right words to break the silence, but nothing came.

• • •

Martin dropped Lucy off at Garza's house. She didn't see any point in playing coy, considering she had already mucked things up with Martin. She was disappointed in herself, how could she have been so sloppy? She should never have gotten him involved.

She waited until Martin left before taking out the key and going inside. Garza stood in the living room. He was visibly annoyed—breathing heavily and glaring.

"What the fuck are you doing?" he asked.

"What?"

Lucy sat on the sofa as Garza stood over her. "It's late as hell. What were you doing all night with this guy?"

"I was getting to know him."

"A date?"

"Yeah, I guess it was."

"Shit. You're so green it's not even funny."

"It wasn't supposed to be a date. I wanted more information on Soto."

"And what did you find out? Where he golfs? His favorite bar? Some fucking place we can bag him and be done with this?"

"No," she said in a low, broken voice.

"What was that?" he asked.

"I didn't get anything we could use."

"Of course, you didn't," Garza said as he threw up his hands, "I knew you weren't ready for this."

Lucy shot up from the sofa and stood eye-to-eye with Garza. "I made a mistake. It won't happen again."

Garza fumed. "I won't let you fuck this up," he said before returning to his room. Lucy went into the backyard and sat with the dogs. She couldn't stop thinking about Martin but knew she needed to keep him at bay.

After giving the dogs a few biscuits, she retired to the sofa for a restless night.

CHAPTER EIGHT

LUCY WOKE TO THE SMELL of Garza cooking breakfast—eggs, bacon and burnt toast. She walked into the kitchen and stood, leaning in the doorway she was like a child checking if her parent was still angry. "You make some for me?" she asked in a timid voice.

"There's enough for you," Garza said.

He buttered his toast and then added a spoonful of grape jam, spreading it over the blackened center. "We'll run the dogs after breakfast," he said.

"Okay."

Lucy made herself a plate and sat down to eat.

"You going to see that kid again?" Garza asked.

"I don't know—I probably shouldn't."

"You ain't got another choice but to see him."

"What do you mean? I thought you didn't want me hanging with him?"

"You got him on the hook and we need to know where they live."

"What do I say? 'Hey, what's your address so I can come

by and kill your pops'?"

"No. we're going to follow him home after he leaves work."

"How do you figure that?"

"Send him one of those text messages. Tell him you want to meet him for dinner when he gets off—some place he'll need a tie for. That way he's sure to go home and get washed up. I'll tail him in the van."

"Just one problem."

"What is it?"

"I don't know any restaurant worth dressing up for."

"Musso and Frank on Sunset."

"Sounds old."

"It is."

Garza dropped his plate into the sink. "I'll be out back," he said.

• • •

After running the dogs, Garza worked on the van while Lucy awaited a response from Martin. It wasn't in her nature to wait to hear from a man. In fact, she had never been in such a position and found it uncomfortable—were there really women out there who held their breaths waiting for men to text or call? How tragic and needy, she thought. Yet, here she was counting the hours until Martin would finally respond.

His text came in the late afternoon. She had all but given up and had dreaded having to tell Garza his plan hadn't worked. Martin agreed to meet her and as Garza anticipated, he planned to go home and get changed after work.

Lucy tapped against the hood of the van, and Garza slid from under the engine. He was covered in oil and holding a wrench. "Dinner is on," she said, "Martin leaves work at five."

"Good. We'll be there." Garza gave an assured grunt and returned to the engine.

● ● ●

Lucy wasn't one for dresses, but she felt the occasion called for it. She took the bus to a department store at a mall in Torrance. She purchased a blue two-toned dress; the cut was refined with a conservative length. She paired it with strappy high-heels and her leather bomber to combat the evening's chill. She couldn't remember the last time she had worn a dress, figuring it was uneventful and so long ago that it was a distant memory.

Garza drove the slow lane on the 405 North, merging onto the 105 West before exiting onto Sepulveda. Garza was quieter than usual. Lucy wondered what was going through his mind—was he still angry about last night? What did he think of her? Had she grown weak in his eyes? Maybe if she could get him talking, she could show him that she was still dedicated—she hadn't gotten cold feet. Sure, Martin was a nice guy, the nicest she had met in a long time, if ever, but his father was a murderer, and nothing was going to change that—nothing.

"He has a motorcycle and tends to drive fast," Lucy said. "You think you'll be able to keep up?"

Garza didn't look at her, and after a long and deliberate breath, he said: "I guess we'll see."

"You changed the oil again?" she asked.

"Tuned her up."

"So, what's the deal with this restaurant tonight—Musso and Frank? Why there?"

"It's a place I used to go."

"How's the food?"

"Good."

"Any recommendations?"

"Try not to fuck him."

Garza's words cut deep, and Lucy didn't speak until they reached Marina Del Rey, and she directed him to the convalescent home. It was 4:45; Martin's motorcycle was parked in front. At 5:10 he came out, put on his helmet and started the bike. He rode South on Lincoln towards Santa Monica. Garza had little trouble following, but the rush hour traffic was beginning to set in. Martin merged onto Pacific Coast Highway and stayed in the left lane to Malibu. With more open road, he began to pick up speed. Garza shifted the gear box and mashed the pedal. The van groaned. There was the smell of burnt oil and exhaust plums steeped in the air.

"You sure this van can keep up?" Lucy asked.

"It ain't no heap."

"I've been on that bike. It's got kick and he knows how to ride it."

"You want to give him a damn medal for it? We'll catch him on the curves."

The curves came, and Martin slowed enough to maneuver, but it was the appearance of a highway patrol cruiser that brought the motorcycle to cruising speed. He made a right turn and headed up a steep hill. Garza was a few car-lengths behind, but he never let Martin dip out of sight. Martin made a series of turns into a residential neighborhood before riding up the driveway of a large white bungalow. Garza parked across the street and watched as Martin entered through the garage.

Despite the state's drought, the lawn was plush, green and manicured. A bed of rose bushes and yellow flowers lined the front of the house. A trail of yard lights along a walkway led to the front door. A sign for a home security company was staked in the ground adjacent to the front door.

"Shit," Lucy said, "they're loaded."

"Welcome to Malibu."

"So, this is where they hide," Lucy said.

"What do you mean?"

"You know…rich people. White people."

Garza watched the house as if to memorize it.

"What are you going to do?" Lucy asked.

"Nothing."

"But you're coming back, aren't you?"

"I'll need to clock the movements of the house—the comings and goings."

"We probably should get to Hollywood before traffic gets worse."

Garza didn't move. He looked as if he didn't want to leave the stakeout. He finally peeled his eyes away and started up the van to drive back the way they came. He drove fast and seemed to have a second sense for cops along the highway. Others would get pulled over for speeding but not Garza; despite the condition of the van and its expired tags, he avoided all suspicion. To a cop or a passerby, he was an old man, perhaps on a job—a gardener, a plumber or painter. The type of man no one would notice—the type that didn't matter. Who would question him in Malibu or the Palisades? He was like the many others—migrant and poor—trying to survive in a city where those who looked like him were invisible. Lucy understood. Garza had grown accustomed to existing in the shadows, but some part of him longed to step into the light. Perhaps to be known again? And for his name to be whispered in the city's darkest corners—Tito Garza and his hounds of hell.

It took forty minutes for Garza to get to Sunset Boulevard. He drove through Westchester and Inglewood. Then, he took La Cienega to Fairfax and stayed north until he reached the long stretch of theaters, bars and nightclubs. Sunset smelt of warmed garbage and piss. Tourists wandered about taking photos of everything in sight—it was all unremarkable. Celebrity impersonators mugged in snapshots for cash in front of the Grauman's Chinese Theater. Garza smirked as a defeated Marilyn Monroe batted down her dress and flaunted her bosom. Onlookers jeered; a group of men mocked her with obscene gestures. Street kids in tatters stood in front of fast-food restaurants begging for change for their fixes. Tour busses and expensive cars, shiny and loud, inched down the street. Garza remembered a time when the cars made the boulevard electric. He loved to watch the sun hit the chrome bumpers and fenders, and the white walled tires against pavement; it was a time of class and elegance.

"This place used to be different," he said.

"You having a moment?"

"Don't be a bitch."

"But you've got free reign to be an asshole?"

"When you get my age, you'll understand. Things don't always change for the better."

"How much longer?"

"It's the next block."

"You can let me out here. I'll walk," Lucy said.

Lucy opened the door before Garza came to a complete stop.

"Just hold on a second," he said.

She jumped out of the van. "I didn't sleep with him and I don't plan on it," she said before slamming the door and slipping into the herd of pedestrians.

● ● ●

The menu at Musso and Frank was steeply priced. Lucy decided on a salad. Martin had steak and potatoes. The dinner was not how Lucy imagined. Martin was quiet; the tension was thick.

"So why did you come?" Lucy asked.

"I don't know. Why did you invite me?"

"I wanted to see you."

"To be honest, I was surprised you bothered."

Martin adjusted his tie, loosening the knot. He sawed through his steak before depositing the rare meat into his mouth. He chewed slowly, and Lucy wondered what to say next.

"I know I messed up," she said, "I'm trying to make it right."

"What is it with you Lucy? Just when I think we're connecting you do a complete one-eighty."

"I'm sorry."

"For what exactly?"

"I got spooked. It's like I told you, it's been a long time. Sometimes I just say and do the wrong things. I see things going one way in my head and then in reality it all goes to shit."

Lucy thought of herself as some teen actress in a romance flick. The type of movie set in a high school without graffiti and metal detectors; where the geeky girl, post makeover and highlights, lands the sensitive jock with her charm and wit. They confess their love to each other at prom and shun all those who fought to keep them apart. It all made Lucy want to upchuck. The conversation was banal, and Martin wore his hurt the way she used to. Inside, he was still the boy who lost his mother and now he had a savior complex. Lucy figured she was the type of damaged girl he thought he could fix. That was the real reason he accepted her invitation, he couldn't bear giving up on her. Or was she a dire cynic and he truly cared?

"Maybe we can hit the reset button? Start fresh?" she said.

"Is that what you actually want?"

"It is."

"Okay."

Martin reached his hand for Lucy to take. She slipped her fingers into his palm. His hands were soft. His pinky was crooked, possibly from being broken at one time. It felt nice being touched by Martin. She left her hand in his for another moment before letting go. When the waiter came, they ordered dessert and lattes.

"I like this place. It reminds me of old Hollywood," he said. "Like something out of a black and white film."

Lucy admired the décor. "Yes, it does have its charm."

"This is your kind of place?" Martin asked.

"No. It was a suggestion."

"Let me guess…from your grandfather?"

"Yes."

"How's he doing? Are you still thinking of placing him at the facility?"

"He's not a fan of living in a place like that but I'm working on changing his mind."

"Maybe you can bring him by to check it out. A lot of times all it takes is a tour and they get on board."

"Yes. Maybe I'll do that."

They finished their apple pie and coffee. Martin left cash and a healthy tip. Outside, night had fallen, and the strip was beginning to come alive with club-goers in skin-tight cocktail dresses and stilettos; they were escorted by frat boy types in muscle shirts and gelled hair.

"You feel like drinks?" Martin asked.

"Not really my scene," she said.

"What is your scene?"

"I don't know. Anywhere but here."

"You don't have a favorite bar or someplace?"

Lucy was quiet as she pulled a smoke from her jacket and lit it.

"Where did you park?" she asked.

"In the back."

"Okay," she said, "I know a place."

• • •

They rode the 101 Freeway and briefly merged onto the 110, exiting on Flower Street; soon they arrived at Lucy's apartment building. Lucy hadn't noticed, but Garza had tailed them the entire way. His van stayed behind a few cars, never overcommitting at the risk of being noticed. It didn't pose a challenge due to slowing traffic and the small compact cars that never hindered his view. There was only once that Garza nearly lost them. Martin had rode between cars, passing a slow-moving truck before getting into the right lane. Garza threw the van into gear, cutting off drivers who honked and shouted, before getting his view back. Garza had breathed a sigh of relief when they finally arrived at a stained brick building. Garza recognized it as an old hotel that was popular in the 1960s—it had been a home away from home for out-of-town bankers. It was a fixture in Bunker Hill and Garza had known two crooked accountants who had set up shop there. The hotel was later converted into apartments sometime in the mid-1980s. Garza couldn't remember what had become of the accountants.

Garza watched as Lucy and Martin stood at the building's entrance. Martin leaned in; Lucy's head was cocked, her lips pursed. The girl had said she had no intention of sleeping with Martin, but Garza couldn't help but think she had truly gone soft. Lucy opened the door and Martin followed her inside. Garza saw a light appear in a corner apartment and bodies moving about. It was all he needed to see. He shifted from neutral; the gear fell into first and he headed back to San Pedro.

• • •

Lucy returned to San Pedro in the morning, entering Garza's house around 7 AM. The sun was budding, golden light splintered through an opening in the curtains. The house was quiet. Garza was sitting on the sofa. He had walked the dogs late into the night and had finally settled into bed around 2 AM, only to wake again three hours later. Lucy had showered and was wearing jeans and a T-shirt. Her hair was still damp; she had it pinned in a bun.

"He drive you here?" Garza asked.

"I took the bus," Lucy said.

A cigarette was burning in the tray on the coffee table. Garza stared at her harshly before getting up and going into the kitchen.

Garza didn't make breakfast, only coffee. He didn't ask Lucy how the night went, and Lucy knew not to speak of it. Over the next two days, they would only mutter a few words to each other. When Lucy would ask about the plan, Garza would say he was still working on it.

When Garza caught her texting on her phone, he'd scoff and walk into the other room. He never mentioned Martin, but knew she was still in communication with him.

Garza's schedule had changed, he woke before sunrise and left the house, returning around 10 AM. Lucy looked after the dogs, running them hard and perfecting the attack commands. Paco had progressed more than Sarge. He had grown vicious and once in a frenzy, he was hard to control. Sarge was generally calm and was patient with his attacks. Once clamped onto her arm or leg, he'd only loosen with a gentle stroke on his snout or by Lucy speaking his name. Then, he'd stand like a sentry awaiting her next command.

It was the third day when Garza spoke to Lucy in full

sentences. She heard a commotion and got up to see about it. Garza was rummaging in the kitchen. He was dressed in a long brown coat and gloves.

"He likes to jog in the mornings," he said abruptly.

"Who?"

"Victor Soto. It's a trail he takes that runs into Will Rogers State Park."

"Parks are busy, aren't they?"

"Not when he goes. The park isn't even open—and he doesn't go through the gates, neither. He runs a dirt road that takes him up into the canyon. That part of the trail is not supposed to be in use, but he jumps the barrier."

"He's alone?"

"Has been the times I've watched him."

"Okay."

"I'm taking Sarge."

"Just one?"

"Paco is too wiry—might call too much attention. I figure Sarge can get to him quieter."

"When do we do it?"

"We'll leave in ten minutes."

• • •

Lucy led Sarge into the back of the van and got settled. She had gloves, a flashlight and Garza's two-way radios in her bag. Hours spent wondering how she'd feel on the day of the deed—she was strangely numb. Perhaps once Soto was dead, she'd feel something? Maybe relief or vindication?

Garza's plan was to reach the trail before Soto. He'd get Sarge setup in the thicket and wait until Soto jogged past. Once he was a few feet out, he'd let Sarge go after him.

Traffic was light driving into Malibu. It was early enough that most people hadn't began their commute to work. The unassuming van traveled along the freeway; its loud clanking engine made Sarge addled. Garza had placed a magnetic decal on the van's side that read: *Harbor Plumbing Co.* Lucy had never seen decals that worked like oversized refrigerator magnets. She explained to Garza that businesses now used custom painted vehicles or wrapping that stuck to the entire car like a sticker.

"Sounds like that'd hurt the paint," he said.

"I think it's pretty safe."

Lucy pulled one of the radios from her bag. "How's the reception on these things?"

"Works fine," he said, "you ever use one before?"

"No."

"You press the top yellow button and speak—simple as that."

Lucy pressed the button; the radio popped and hissed.

"A little feedback, that's all," Garza said.

"How long do you think it'll take for him to get up the trail to where you'll be?" she asked.

"Once you see him, say it over the radio. After that, I figure we'll sit tight for five to six minutes. I'll let the dog loose after he gets a good distance. The dog has a soft step and if he's moving fast, he'll get a good jump on Soto."

They parked on a residential cul-de-sac. At the end was the gated entrance to the park. A small booth for a parking attendant was empty. Garza had spent days surveying the location and knew what time the park rangers and attendants arrived. Later in the day, buses of school children on field trips would line the street awaiting entry. And before that, husbands and wives would drive their luxury cars down driveways as gardeners blew leaves and cut grass, and nannies pushed baby strollers down sidewalks. It was another world, far from the one Garza had known—a fairy-tale conjured of the well-to-dos. He was close once, to getting a piece of the pie. But that seemed like ages ago, his dreams vanquished every hour spent in a prison cell.

Times like these, before a kill, he would remember his love, Maria. How she would get a look in her eye when he'd come home knowing that he'd done a terrible thing. Her touch, warm and soft, against the wet clamminess of his skin. Cupping his face with her hands, she'd look into his eyes and whisper, "God bless your eyes, *Marido*—you've still got your soul in there."

When he was finally released from prison, the divorce had been finalized. The last time Maria looked into his eyes; it was as if their once passionate love never happened. He watched her load her things into a rented moving truck; his eyes were seared with sorrow. Something inside of him was gone, maybe his last vestige of humanity? And from that day forward, he never second guessed a hit. He killed indiscriminately, and no amount of begging and tearful pleas of mercy could sway him. If he was sent for you, you were dead.

The dog led Garza down the road and up the stony trail. Lucy watched with radio in hand until they were out of sight, and then got back into the van. Garza huddled in the bushes. He stroked between Sarge's ears and waited.

A German roadster stopped at the base of the street. Victor Soto climbed out of the low sitting car and opened his trunk. He removed a backpack and slipped his arms through the straps. He began to jog up the street. He passed Lucy, who was crouched on the van floor, but managed to see him approaching in the side-view mirror.

She pushed the button on the radio. "He's coming now," she said.

"All right," Garza said, "we're ready."

Victor had found trail running later in life but as a

consummate athlete, he took to it with ease. He had made a name for himself while at Stanford as a linebacker and was an All-American shot-putter. Even though Victor carried some extra weight, at fifty he was still able to run a five-minute mile. He had hoped trail running would absolve the six years he spent damaging himself with booze, cigarettes and late nights in casinos, anything to avoid being home. The house had become like a hospital. It was around-the-clock care for his wife: nurses, doctors, and the chaplain on standby. The house was filled with the odor of the caustic fluid his wife had to pump from her gut twice a day. Through a tube drawn from a port-a-catheter, she willed the fluid into a bucket on the floor—two-hundred milliliters of blood and bile. She was gaunt, all but her distended stomach that had swollen three times its normal size.

Victor neared a bend in the trail that led to an incline. He pumped feverishly until he reached the top, sprinting past Garza and Sarge who had taken up in the bushes. Garza watched methodically, his hand gripped the collar and hair of the dog's neck. He whispered to Sarge; the dog lowered his head and raised his shoulders. Sarge shifted his weight forward and tugged. Garza released him. The dog sprang from the bushes, hitting the trail and racing after Victor.

Garza tried to stay hidden but needed to confirm the kill. It had been over a decade since he watched a dog rip the flesh from a man's bones. It was like viewing an invasive operation—surgical yet grotesque.

When Sarge reached Victor, he dug his teeth into Victor's right calf, causing him to stumble. Victor's agonizing wail echoed along the trail. He shirked, pivoting on his left foot and then faced the dog. Blood spurted into the dirt. Victor cursed and pulled his backpack around to his chest. He dug inside the pack until he produced a small pistol. Sarge growled and heaved his head about until he ripped open Victor's calf. Slender muscled tissue peeled down the leg like corn husk. Seeing the gun, Garza crawled from the bushes and began running down the trail. Victor began to fire, wildly, sending bullets down the trail and narrowly missing Sarge whose darting kept him from a sure shot. The shots were loud and echoed along the trail. Sarge released Victor and he stumbled to the ground. The dog's teeth had scraped bone; the type of pain that can send the body into shock.

Garza looked back to see Victor on the ground and Sarge repositioning to seize his throat, exactly how he had trained him. Soon it would be over, Garza thought as he kept moving down the trail. Lucy called over the radio.

"What's happening?" she asked.

"I'm running," Garza said, out of breath.

"Why the hell are you running?"

"Start the van," he said.

Lucy did as she was told. Garza scuttled, nearly losing his footing and dropping the radio. When he had reached the road's end, two gunshots sent birds flying from the treetops. He stopped and looked back toward the trail. He blew the dog whistle.

Lucy rolled down the window. "What the hell was that?" she asked, "Where is Sarge?"

Garza blew the whistle again—harder, longer, but the dog didn't come.

"Shit," he said, "Fucker shot him."

"Soto's alive?"

"I don't know."

"Should you check?" Lucy asked, "And what about Sarge?"

Garza shook his head. "It's too risky to go back now."

"Shit. We need to get out of here," Lucy said.

She jumped into the passenger's seat as Garza got into the

van. Garza jerked the wheel, making a U-turn, and then sped down the street. He was questioning the mission. Perhaps he had taken on too much? He knew killing an A.D.A wouldn't be easy, but things were going to hell fast. He wanted to turn back for the dog, but he knew the risk was too great. It was likely Sarge didn't survive the shooting, but he hoped the dog had nicked an artery and Soto would bleed out before the EMTs could go to work on him. But if Soto survived, they would have to wait a good while before their next attempt, a few weeks or even a month, until things cooled down. The job was only done when Soto was on a slab in the morgue, but at what cost? Garza had convinced himself that saving Sarge and Paco, giving them a new purpose, was better than a life in the kennel or being put down when no one adopted them. He thought he had spared them from an inevitable death, but death found Sarge anyway, and Garza knew it was his fault. Garza was without a conscious, but he did have a code, and it meant never leaving a 'man' behind.

CHAPTER NINE

GARZA LIT A SMOKE. "He's going to survive. If he were dead, we'd know by now," he said matter-of-fact. He paced the living room as Lucy sat on the sofa watching the news.

"Who the fuck carries a gun on a hiking trail?" she asked.

Garza snickered. "I should have known he'd have a piece."

"Why?"

"Because any man with a past like his wouldn't be caught without protection."

"More shit we have to shovel," Lucy said.

"We'll be better prepared next time. We can't afford not to be."

"You ever get caught out there? I mean someone almost put one in your ass?" Lucy asked.

"Not me but others I knew. There was a man—some nobody who had slept with a made guy's wife. He kept a twenty-two on him all the time. Some guys had been sent to take care of him. When they finally caught him, he put two fellas down before catching a bullet in the noggin. These guys he put down were enforcers, but they had underestimated him. And they paid for it."

"We'll be more careful."

"Soto will be on high alert. Even if he figures it was a random dog loose on the trail, the whole thing is enough to shake him up. He'll be watching his back."

"Since when is an A.D.A. getting attacked by a dog not news?" Lucy asked as she turned the knob on the TV. "They report on trivial shit, but an A.D.A. nearly dying doesn't make it?"

"It's not news because he doesn't want it to be."

"What about the cops?"

"They will buy whatever he tells them."

"Shit," she said, "I thought we had him for sure."

"We'll get him," Garza said, "we wait until things settle and give it another shot."

"Poor Sarge. I can't believe we just left him like that."

"We didn't have a choice."

"Yeah, but he would never have been in that mess had it not been for us."

"Let it go."

"How? I mean don't tell me you don't feel something. He was our friend."

"I buried my last friend on the beach. Sarge wasn't a friend, he was a soldier—a means to an end. What I feel is tired, frustrated, angry but I ain't the sentimental type."

Lucy's phone vibrated. She picked it up and ran her thumb across the screen.

"It's a text from Martin…he wants me to meet him at the hospital. Soto is going to have surgery on his leg."

"Which hospital?"

"Cedars."

"I'll take you," Garza said.

• • •

When they arrived at the hospital, police cars were stationed in front. Officers stood drinking coffee and talking. Lucy got out of the van.

"You coming back to get me?" she asked.

"There's a coffee shop around the corner. Meet me there after you're done with Soto and the boy."

"What's the shop called?"

"The sign says *Coffee and Donuts*—shouldn't be too hard."

Lucy rolled her eyes. "Whatever."

Lucy kept her head down as she passed the officers. No one paid her much attention until she approached the information desk and asked what room Victor Soto was in. Looking somewhat out of place, Lucy got the attention of a man who looked to be a plain clothed detective dressed in a short-sleeved shirt and wrinkled khakis.

"Who are you?" the man asked.

"I'm a friend of Martin. He asked me to come," she said.

"Like a school friend?"

"No. Like a girlfriend."

"What's your name?"

"Lucy."

"You have I.D.?"

Lucy took her I.D. card from her pocket and handed it to the detective. He looked it over and dialed on his cell phone. He told the voice on the other end that Lucy was there at Martin's request. The detective listened as the voice relayed information and then ended the call.

"You can follow me," he said handing her I.D. back.

Lucy followed the detective into an elevator marked for hospital personnel. He pushed the button for the third floor.

"Don't use this elevator when you come down," he said,

"take the others."

"Okay."

"Girlfriend you say?"

"Yes."

"Interesting."

"Is that a problem?" Lucy asked.

"You work together or something?"

"I don't see how any of that is your business."

The detective smiled. The elevator opened, and Lucy followed him to the room. The detective knocked on the door.

"I can take it from here," Lucy said.

The detective ignored her and waited until Martin opened the door and stepped into the hallway.

"You came," Martin said, "I wasn't sure you would." He threw his arms around her. When they broke their embrace, Lucy glared at the detective who was still standing next to them.

"We're good, Jim," Martin said.

Jim nodded and headed back toward the elevator.

"What's with him?" Lucy asked.

"He's a friend of my dad's and like an uncle to me. He used to be cop, now I think he just does favors for my dad. He can be a little overprotective."

"How are you doing?"

"I'm okay," Martin said.

"And your dad?"

"Worst luck ever, but the surgeon says he can repair the damage and he'll be back on his feet in a few months or so."

"You said a dog attacked him?"

"Pretty gnarly, huh?"

"Like a stray?" she asked.

"Maybe. They think it could have been someone's pet that got lose and started living up there. They checked if it had a microchip but there's no identification or anything."

"What about the dog? They check for rabies?"

"Luckily it was rabies free. My dad had to put two rounds in him—he's pretty upset about it. He's got a soft spot for dogs."

Lucy swallowed hard as she thought about Sarge.

"Is he in surgery?"

"Not yet. They'll prep him in an hour. He was snoozing—he's on some pretty strong pain killers. He woke up a few minutes ago. You want to meet him?"

Lucy hesitated. She could feel moisture form in the bends of her arms, and there was a tightness in her chest.

"Shit. I did it again, didn't I?" Martin said. "Sorry, we're supposed to be taking this slow. You should meet him when you're ready."

"No. It's okay. I came all this way. I can meet him."

"You sure?"

"Why not?"

"Okay," Martin said.

Martin opened the door and Lucy followed him inside the room. Victor was in a gown lying still with an I.V. in his right arm. A tray of untouched food was next to the bed, along with a cup of ice chips and a foam water pitcher.

"Dad, you didn't eat," Martin said.

"Food is shit."

"At least drink some water."

"I'm getting all the water I need through this damn thing," he said looking to the hanging saline bag.

"I want you to meet a friend," Martin said.

"I didn't know we had company," Victor said peering at Lucy as she moved from behind Martin.

"Hello, Mister Soto."

Victor extended his hand and Lucy walked toward him. Looking at his open palm, she wondered how his hands looked touching her mother's body—did the veins flare and knuckles bulge when he exercised his grip around her arms, wrists or neck? Was it his hands balled into fists that sent tremors throughout her body with each punch?

She would sooner die than touch him. But Martin's face shone with pride; his eyes bright and dopey. If only he knew what his father truly was, he would no longer be that sweet boy in the dark; he'd know there were monsters in the world—monsters like his father.

How easy it would be to kill Soto as he lay in bed, feeble. If she had her switchblade, she could run it down his arm or along his neck. She'd watch his life slip away with each breath. And as Soto clung to his last bit of life, she'd whisper into his ear her mother's name.

Martin would mourn him for a time but after a while, he'd accept the truth. He would know what his father was, and he would see how Victor Soto set everything into motion. He'd see that there was no other way—no turning a blind-eye—not when it was Lucy's mother. They both had mourned their mothers and knew it was a pain that cut deep.

Lucy touched Victor's hand. His skin felt thick and cold. She couldn't bear eye contact, so she focused on his ear.

"And who do we have here?"

"I'm Lucy."

"It's a pleasure to meet you," Soto said.

"Likewise, Mr. Soto. Sorry to hear about your leg."

She released his hand and then shoved it into her pocket.

"Oh well, what can you do? I'm just glad I walked away from it."

Lucy nodded and turned to Martin. "I should get going," she said.

"I'll walk you out," Martin said.

He reached over, touching his father's shoulder. "I'll be

back a little later."

"I'll be here," Victor said, "take care, Lucy."

"Likewise, sir."

"Call me Victor. In fact, when I'm out of this place you should come over for a barbecue. How's that sound?"

"Sounds nice," she said.

"Great."

Martin followed Lucy out of the room. They stood silently by the door, before he leaned in, pressing his lips against hers. She pulled away slightly—her face shone a rooted shame.

"We okay?" Martin asked.

"Why wouldn't we be?"

"No reason, I guess—just checking in."

"We're fine, Martin. I'll see you later, okay?"

"Okay."

Lucy left Martin idling in the hallway. There was a current of unease. He watched until Lucy exited through the double-doors. Lucy never looked back and Martin didn't have the guts to follow her.

Lucy walked to the coffee shop to meet Garza. He had already drunk two cups of black and consumed a cake doughnut, chocolate glaze had smudged his lower lip. She sat down across from him.

"I met him," she said, "Soto."

"He as bad off as we hoped?" Garza asked.

"He'll survive. He's got a surgery scheduled."

"Tell me about him? What type of man is he?"

"Everything he said felt rehearsed. But Martin is his fanboy. I saw it in his eyes."

"Sons can be like that. Hopefully he won't get in our way."

"He won't. I'll make sure of it."

"I have no problem digging two graves."

"You already made that clear."

"You want coffee or something?"

"I'm fine."

"We should get back to San Pedro before traffic hits." Garza wiped his mouth and then readied himself to leave.

"He invited me to a barbecue," Lucy blurted.

"A barbecue?"

"Yes. Victor invited me to his home."

Garza slipped back into his chair and rested his arms on the table. Lucy was pensive.

"It could be an opportunity," he said, "maybe slip something in his drink? Make it nice and clean."

"Like what?"

"Ricin. Cyanide. Nicotine maybe?" he said in a low voice.

"You can get your hands on all that?"

"Yes."

Garza stood up and headed for the door. Lucy gathered herself and followed. They began walking to the van, which was parked in a small lot adjacent to the coffee shop.

"Poison makes me nervous," she said.

"Why is that?"

"Because I'm the one doing it. The risk is all on me."

"You want him dead, don't you?"

"What if I fuck it up? Maybe I don't put enough? He smells it, or it tastes funny?"

"The poisons I use are odorless and tasteless. There's no way he'd know."

They got into the van and Garza started the engine.

"It's all risk, Lucita. No matter how it's done," he said.

● ● ●

It took them twenty minutes to get to San Pedro. When they reached Gaffey Street, they followed a large construction truck into the neighborhood. It parked in front of the house where the boys died; the property was now crawling with workers. Men hammered away on the roof and cleared the dead bushes from in front of the house. A white man stood in pressed khakis, a polo shirt and a hard hat, shouting to the men on the roof. A clipboard was in his left hand and a large soda in the other.

"Someone bought that shit-hole?" Lucy said. "They must have gotten a deal."

Garza grunted disapprovingly.

"How much you think it went for?" Lucy asked.

"Bank probably bought it for pennies on the dollar and then auctioned it off."

"Damn gringos. They are smart, man. He's probably going to flip that shit for a pretty penny."

"Probably," Garza said.

Garza pulled into the garage and let the van settle. Lucy opened the door and moved to get out; Garza grabbed her arm.

"You saw the man you're going to kill today."

"Yeah."

"So? What did you feel?"

"It's like I told you."

"I'm talking about that gut feeling—it's more of a physical reaction."

Lucy took a moment to gather her thoughts. "He made me sick. Knowing what he did and then being so close to him—it all made me want to hurt him more."

"You'll get your chance, again."

"I've waited this long, a little longer won't hurt. What's for dinner?"

"Thought it might be a good day to grill," Garza said, "I got a few T-bones in the freezer and Paco can have the scraps."

After dinner, Lucy wrapped the bones in foil and took them out to Paco. She gave him the bones and sat outside with him for a while. He'd whimper periodically, looking at where Sarge had once laid. Sarge's absence had sparked a change in Paco. He had grown less respondent and more unpredictable. Sarge was never far from Lucy's thoughts, but for Garza he seemed to be a fleeting memory. Was Garza really that cold? Lucy knew he was capable of love—he had a family and he cared for Gazpacho. But Garza had killed so many people and when he spoke of his crimes, he was cavalier and even prideful. Garza was a monster and Lucy knew what he was capable of, but somewhere inside, perhaps there still existed a decent man and if so, Lucy feared there wasn't much of that decency left.

Paco chomped on his bone as Lucy stroked between his ears. Before going into the house, she walked over to a stick pile and picked up two twigs, fashioning them together to make a cross. She laid the cross on the ground where Sarge had worked the grass to dirt. She lit a cigarette and smoked it. Afterwards, she went into the house to sleep.

• • •

With each passing day, Lucy awaited word from Martin about his father. They texted periodically but the conversations didn't extend past mundane hellos and quick check-ins. Garza kept himself occupied, finally cleaning up the filthy house—dusting, sweeping, and raking dead leaves and trash outside. When he wasn't cleaning, he was clipping articles from his newspapers and organizing them into bags—a system only he understood. They both worked with Paco, teaching him new commands—he was becoming more efficient, but he maintained a wily nature and no amount of training seemed to calm him.

It was midweek, late in the day, when Garza was rinsing off the side of his house. Dirt had dried and was layered thick; the integrity of the paint was in jeopardy. He didn't want to have to paint the house, though it needed it. The last time it had been painted was over ten years ago. For Garza, the house was a place to store junk and sleep. But since Lucy had arrived, he began seeing it more as a home. It was a place to live and plot—he imagined them planning future hits, counting their earnings, performing an inventory of poisons and weapons. With time, he thought, Lucy could be one of the best. The type of killer no one would expect; she could blend into any setting, getting close to her marks. She was intelligent—smarter than he was at her age—and her face was cause for more than a passing glance. Garza thought, with some effort, Lucy could be a looker, and her beauty would be a weapon. She could be taught to use her looks and charm the way Garza learned to handle a blackjack.

Garza dropped a pile of crumbling leaves into a black trash bag. When he heard footsteps, he turned to see a white man in shorts and a UCLA t-shirt jogging in place listening to earbuds. The man took a smart phone from his pocket, tapping the screen quickly and smiling.

"Sorry, I forget I have this thing on sometimes…"

"What do you want?" Garza asked.

"Sorry. Taylor Barnes. I'm overseeing some construction in the neighborhood," he said.

"Yeah, the house with all the workers?"

"That's right," Taylor said. "Sorry about the racket. It should all be done this week."

"What all you got going on?"

"Phase one is replacing the roof and some plumbing."

"You mind me asking how much you bought it for?"

"Let's just say, it was a hell of a deal. Word is it was

marked down because of some crime that happened. Something about the past owners being attacked by coyotes. How bizarre is that? You ever hear of such a thing?"

"I tend to keep to myself."

"That's probably a good thing. This neighborhood has had its share of problems but we're going to change all that."

"How?"

"By investing in the community. Have you lived here long?"

Garza had stopped raking and was looking at Taylor intensely. "For a while now."

"Well, you're in store for some great changes. I'm talking a light rail system from here to downtown—skyrise apartments, boutique shopping centers, gourmet markets—the works."

"What did you say your name was?" Garza asked.

"Taylor Barnes."

"Barnes," Garza repeated, "Like Tina Barnes?"

"You've met my wife?"

"Came by with some baked goods. She said you were living in Jorge's old place."

"Just until it's ready to go back on the market. We like to live in the neighborhood we're revitalizing—it's how we get a flavor for the place and really figure out what it needs."

Taylor pulled a business card from his pocket. "Here you go," he said, "and what's your name, sir?"

"Ramirez."

"Mister Ramirez. It's a pleasure. I'd shake your hand but I'm sweating like a pig."

"Don't trouble yourself."

"I better get back to my run and enjoy this beautiful L.A. weather we're having."

"Yeah," Garza said, "sure."

Taylor sprinted down the alley. The business card read: The Phoenix Group. Garza sighed as he put the card into his pocket.

• • •

In the kitchen, Garza poured a cold glass of water and wiped the sweat from his forehead with a rag. He guzzled the water and then poured more.

"Damn heat," he said.

Lucy entered from the garage carrying a box of dog treats. Her body pads were stained with grass and dirt.

"I ran through the last of the commands you wanted him to learn," she said.

"How'd he do?" Garza asked.

"Took a while but once he got it..."

"He's sharp—more than Sarge was, anyway."

"What'd you have against Sarge, anyway?"

"Nothing but we've all got expiration dates."

"That's how you think of them, isn't it?" Lucy asked, "not dogs but tools you use?"

"I respect them, but they've got a job to do."

"Sarge was a good dog and we left him there. I don't care what you say, it wasn't right."

"You saying we should have gone back for a shot-up mutt? We'd be sitting in a prison cell right now."

Lucy hesitated. "He deserved better than what he got."

"You don't risk getting pinched for nobody, not even your best dog. *Comprende*?"

"I get it—it's still fucked up, though."

"I never said you had to like it but you best figure things out. Get yourself a code and live by it. It'll keep you alive and out of prison."

There was a hard knock at the door. Lucy and Garza stood silent. Garza took a chopping knife from the kitchen drawer and cautiously approached the door. He looked through the peephole and then quickly crouched down.

"Shit," he said.

"Who is it?" Lucy asked.

"Damn neighbor. The gringo who is working on the dead boys' house—he's the husband of the Tina broad that came by."

"You hit on her or something?"

"Not my type."

"Then what's he doing here?" Lucy asked.

"Don't know."

There was another knock. Lucy was getting anxious and Garza had tightened the grip on the blade.

"You going to open up? Doesn't look like this fool is going away," she said.

"Damn," Garza said lowering the knife to his side and unlocking the door. He opened it a crack and revealed Taylor Barnes in tapered denim and a collared shirt. He was holding a plate of cookies covered in plastic wrap.

"I hate to bother you but it's for a worthy cause," Taylor said.

"That right?"

"My wife wanted me to bring these over. It's a plate of her award-winning double-chocolate chip cookies—they took top prize at the Orange County Fair last year."

Garza fought back the urge to slam the door in his face and took the cookies from his hand. "First place?"

"That's right," Taylor said, "and they're gluten and sugar-free. My wife said she thought that you would appreciate something a little healthier than the brownies."

"What's gluten?"

Taylor laughed. "I knew you had a sense of humor in there somewhere."

"Like a sugar substitute or something?"

"Oh, you're serious? No. It's a wheat enzyme, I think. A lot of people are allergic to it."

"Allergic to wheat?"

"Well, yes," Taylor said, "it's become pretty common."

Paco was barking and ready for dinner, having worked off the few treats Lucy had given him during the training session.

"Sounds like you've got a pup on your hands," Taylor said.

"What?"

"He's got a young bark. I grew up with dogs. I've always been good about figuring out the young ones from the older ones by their barks."

"Some talent."

"More of a quirk. Not something I could take on the road, though. What breed do you have?"

"A Pit."

"Great dogs. I mean who needs a security system with a dog like that?"

"I always say a good dog and a shotgun goes a long way."

"I like that," Taylor said smiling. "Enjoy the cookies, Mister Ramirez."

"I'm sure I will."

Garza shut the door and Lucy appeared from the kitchen. "Looks like you've got yourself a BFF."

"What the hell is that?" Garza asked.

"Best-friend-forever."

"Guy is a cancer," Garza said, "he's going to make this neighborhood look like fucking Westwood. If he shows up again, I'll deal with him."

"We can't kill everybody, you know?"

"I didn't say I'd kill him. There are other ways to get a point across."

Lucy's phone vibrated with a text. She picked it up. "We're back on," she said.

"What is it?"

"Martin says Soto's recovered. He invited me to a party to celebrate."

"Good—it's time we finish this."

"How?"

"You'll be able to get close…"

"Poison?"

"With the right amount, it'll look like a medical thing. With his recent surgery, the doctors will be hemmed up trying to figure out what went wrong. By then, you'll be gone."

"Where am I supposed to go?"

"Shit if I know—you just disappear."

"What would I tell Martin? If I just leave, he'd be sure to suspect something."

"Tell him you're going out of town and then lose his number. I told you it was bad business to get involved with that kid."

"I've never been out of L.A. I wouldn't know what to do."

"You go to Union Station and buy a ticket for the next train leaving and you don't look back. After a few years, you come back to the state with a new identity. Maybe you take up in the north near San Jose or Sacramento. Or even out east in San Bernadino—the type of place where people go to be left alone."

"A few years in someplace I don't know?"

"You'll survive. I did. Then, when everyone has forgotten your name, you slip back into L.A. By then, people would have forgotten you. Of course, it won't be the same—nothing ever is."

"I guess I didn't think of what I'd do after Soto was dead."

"You should because once he's dead, everything changes. You never know where suspicion will fall. The best way to make sure it doesn't fall on you is to not be there."

"Shit," Lucy said, "I've never even been on a train before."

"When is the party?" Garza asked.

"This weekend."

"Good. That gives us time to prepare."

CHAPTER TEN

SOTO CHANGED CHANNELS with the remote until reaching a broadcast of track and field—he watched longingly as the runners sprinted around the track. He would have to learn to move like that again. Walking would take some time, but running how he had, that could take years.

Eventually, the excitement faded to melancholy. He turned off the TV and he resigned himself to the quiet. A nurse entered the room and took a seat on the bed. She began massaging his legs with warm oil.

"How's that feel?" she asked.

"Don't be afraid to go deeper," Soto said.

The nurse continued massaging gently.

"It's too soon," she said. "You're still healing."

"But I feel strong—they're releasing me tomorrow. My son is throwing me a welcome back party."

"That's wonderful. I'm glad."

"It's funny how things happen—one minute I'm doing something I love and couldn't imagine living without. The next, I'm in a hospital bed with a doctor telling me that that one thing I thought I couldn't live without, is the exact thing that's been taken away."

"You'll run again, Mister Soto. I'm sure of it."

"No offense, miss. But you don't know a damn thing."

The nurse stopped massaging as she grew uncomfortable. Soto's eyes had ceased blinking and his face was absent of emotion.

"It's just another thing in this world that I've lost," he said.

"Well, I'm sorry you feel that way."

"Feeling sorry isn't going to change it."

"It's a hospital Mister Soto," she said, "There are worst people off here than you."

"You say that like it's supposed to mean something."

The nurse wiped her hands on a cloth she had draped over her shoulder.

"I think this massage is over," she said.

She covered Soto's legs with the sheet and left.

Soto struck his leg with his fists, repeatedly, but his leg didn't respond. There was significant nerve damage. He couldn't bring himself to tell Martin the extent of his injuries. The boy had already gone through so much with his mother, and now his father faced the prospect of being a cripple.

Lucy struggled to decide if Soto's welcome home party called for a dress, or if faded denim cut-offs would do. She needed to look the part as the doting girlfriend, but truthfully Lucy didn't care what she wore, as long as she could conceal the poison she'd be packing. Lucy wondered if she'd be able to dilute the poison enough to kill Soto without causing alarm. Would he convulse and expire quickly? Or would his death be prolonged—taking ten or fifteen minutes— enough time for him to get to the hospital? What if Garza was wrong and Soto could detect the poison right away?

And if so, would Soto quickly shift suspicion to Lucy—the one person who doesn't belong. Garza had assured Lucy the poison was undetectable, but he was an old man, and maybe he couldn't be certain. Overtime, memories can fail, and information can get mixed up like cards shuffled in a deck. He could have gotten his poisons confused and she could be stuck in a house with a detective piecing together why the A.D.A. is once again at death's door.

Lucy decided to wear faded jeans and a button-down blouse. She left the top buttons unfastened, allowing the fabric to spread above where her breasts cleaved. It would be a much-needed distraction for Martin and the rest of the men in the house—anything to keep them from recognizing her as a threat.

Before leaving the house, Garza gave Lucy an expensive bottle of red wine and the vile of poison. She placed the poison in her pocket and blew the dust off the wine bottle.

"How old is this? It's filthy."

"I've been holding on to it for a while," Garza said.

"I can believe that. What was the occasion?"

"It was a wedding gift."

"You sure you want those assholes to drink it? I can always pick up a cheap bottle of Scotch."

"No, Soto will be more impressed by this. We need him to think highly of you."

"Okay."

"We should go. You don't want to be late."

● ● ●

Garza and Lucy drove to Malibu. Traffic was heavy at times and the two hardly spoke—Lucy held the wine bottle in her lap. From the passenger seat, she peered into luxury car windows, something she often did when she rode the bus.

Looking in on someone, watching them carry on—smoking, texting, putting on mascara—she wondered what terrible secrets they harbored. Who had they hurt? Who had hurt them? Who were they planning to hurt? When a person would look at her, having felt her stare, it would be dismissive, and she'd be reminded it was more than a barrier of metal and glass between them—they were worlds apart. In those moments, Lucy longed to vanish—to dissipate into the pervading light of the California sun. The drivers' lack of acknowledgment made Lucy feel like she held no value. It was palpable proof that the wealthy of Los Angeles existed in a bubble. It was an invisible barricade allowing them to see the troubles of the poor while remaining untouched by them. It was the world that Victor and Martin inhabited, and the party would be the closest Lucy would ever get to being inside the bubble.

Garza parked a few blocks away from Soto's house in the most remote section of street he could find. Lucy got out of the van and began walking toward the home. Martin's motorcycle and expensive cars were parked in the driveway.

Lucy rang the doorbell. Martin answered—he wore his signature wide smile and ruddiness.

"You made it," Martin said.

"I wouldn't miss it for anything."

"Come on in."

Lucy followed Martin into the kitchen. Everything was white and spotless. The appliances looked expensive, they were the large metal ones Lucy had only seen in TV commercials and cooking shows but could never imagine someone purchasing. The entire house looked staged for a home magazine photoshoot.

Soto appeared on crutches with Jim by his side. Lucy knew Jim was already suspicious of her since their meeting at the hospital. She knew she'd need to keep her distance. Jim would likely pry her with questions which she'd need to carefully evade.

"Lucy. I'm so glad you came," Victor said. "Forgive me if I don't shake your hand. It takes everything in me to stay upright on these things."

"Its fine, Mister Soto. It's nice to see you getting around."

"It takes more than a dog bite to keep me down."

"I brought you a token—not sure if you're a wine drinker."

Lucy handed Victor the bottle. He examined it closely and smiled.

"Aren't you full of surprises? You must have paid a pretty penny for this."

"I got it from a friend of mine. He's something of a collector."

"Really? I wouldn't mind meeting him. As rare as this is, I'd love to see what else he's keeping."

"How rare?" Lucy asked.

"We're talking maybe fifty bottles produced—all coming from a winery in Geyserville. Rumor was it was owned by some old school mobsters—Vegas casino types. Who is this friend of yours?"

"Just a guy I know," Lucy said, "he's nobody, really."

Victor turned to Martin. "You mind putting this in the wine chiller?"

Martin took the bottle from his father and put it in a small compartment in the refrigerator.

"Feel like a beer, Lucy?" Martin asked.

"Water is fine."

"Water? You sure?"

"Yes."

Martin took a beer and a bottle of water from the refrigerator and swung it shut. He handed the water to Lucy and flipped the beer cap into the trashcan.

"Dinner will be ready soon," Victor said. "Jim is a hell of a grill master. I hope you like meat because you're in for the best baby back ribs you've ever had in your life."

Lucy gave a polite nod and Victor and Jim headed out to the patio where Jim tended to slabs of meat on a smoking rack.

"I thought you were a vegetarian?"

"Not exactly," Lucy said.

"If you don't want to eat it, don't feel like you have too. I stashed a kale salad and some humus in the fridge."

"A little pig won't kill me."

"I'm glad you're here."

"You thought I'd stand you up?"

"I don't know. Things have just been weird with us lately."

"Weird?"

"Distant."

"I figured you needed some space with your dad recovering and everything."

"No, it's cool. I understand—just making sure we're good."

"I'm here," Lucy said, "so we're good."

Martin leaned in to kiss her. Lucy's first instinct was to retreat. She took a step backward but then relented, taking Martin by the hand and placing it on her lower back. She broke away from the embrace to see Victor and Jim watching them through the sliding glass doors.

"Damn," Martin said.

"What's wrong?" Lucy asked.

"Nothing. That was nice—I've missed it."

"Your dad and his friend are scoping us."

Martin looked to his father; whose face bared an expression of gladness.

"We can take the drinks upstairs," Martin said as Lucy

followed him out of the kitchen.

• • •

In the van, Garza listened to a radio broadcast of sports highlights and drank from a flask of gin that he kept stored in the glove compartment. He wondered what was going on inside Soto's home. How was Lucy faring? Was she keeping her cool? Had she managed to slip the poison into the wine? And if so, was Victor enjoying his last few moments of decadence? After all, Victor was leaving the world on top. He was the type of man the city would name a freeway after. Men like Soto were all too common for Garza—brown skinned men with last names that echoed a migrant heritage but denied the Mexican blood that coursed through their veins—a genealogy tucked neatly in the past. It was nothing more than a familial link nearly erased by education and money. Those ancestors with calloused hands that made their lives in fields were distant memories trampled by progress. Garza saw Victor as the worst type of man—the type who'd deny his blood if it suited his agenda. Garza would be glad when Victor was dead—he'd be one less sold-out *pocho*.

• • •

When dinner was served, it was presented on a long platter on the patio table. Ribs, sausage and chicken were stacked high, juicy and slathered in a burgundy sauce. Lucy had never seen that much meat. It made her think of cavemen that stalked the wilderness killing and eating whatever they found, cooking and bestowing it for the entire village. Soto sat at the head of the table with Jim on his right side. Lucy and Martin sat together. At times, Martin would rest his hand on Lucy's thigh—she didn't mind, though she knew she ought to. Martin had become a liability, there was no doubting that. And if Garza could see what was happening between them, he would kill them both. As much as Lucy wanted to, she couldn't dismiss her feelings for him. Hidden behind her anger for Victor, was a dream that she and Martin could be together. It was a fantasy she kept in a locked room.

"I bet the wine is chilled now," Lucy said brushing Martin's hand from her thigh.

Martin was taken aback and sunk into his seat.

"I completely forgot," Victor said, "Martin, you mind grabbing that bottle of wine? I think the ocassion calls for a toast."

"Sure," Martin said as he prepared to get up.

"Allow me," Lucy said, "I know how long to let it breathe."

"Not just a pretty face, I see. The girl knows how a merlot should be treated. There's a wine opener on the counter," Victor said.

Lucy excused herself from the table and went into the kitchen. She took the bottle from the refrigerator and searched for the wine opener. She wasn't surprised when she came upon a small appliance that could mechanically remove the cork. She placed the bottle in the machine and watched as it gently pulled the cork until popping and releasing a rich aroma. In that moment, Lucy understood why Garza had given it to her to serve. There would be no chance of Soto detecting the poison under the smell of the wine's full body. She poured three glasses, varying the amounts in each. The glass with the most wine would go to Soto. She took the cap off the vile and emptied the powder into Soto's glass. She swirled the wine around in the glass making sure the powdered residue was washed clean from the sides. When she was sure the poison had completely mixed, she carried the glasses out to the men who were eagerly waiting.

She handed Soto the poisoned glass and gave the other

two to Martin and Jim.

"Thank you, sweetie."

Lucy returned to her seat and watched as Soto held the glass in preparation of a toast. In a moment, it would all be over. Soto would drink the wine and begin to feel warm like the onset of a fever. His skin would flush, and his heart would pump rapidly, sending additional blood to his extremities. Gradually he'd go into cardiac arrest. Jim and Martin would rush to his aid, maybe apply CPR—chest compressions, controlled breaths. It would all be in vain. And as they would pound on his chest cursing and crying out to God not to let the bastard die, Lucy would rush into the kitchen under the pretense of calling 911; then, she'd leave as she came, walking out of the front door with the wine bottle in hand and brimming with pride—yes, it would all be over then, and Lucy would be free.

Victor cleared his throat and began his speech: "The last few months have been pretty challenging. Who would have thought we'd be making one of the largest real-estate deals in Los Angeles history—and it only took eight years."

Jim and Martin laughed. Lucy tried her best to join in, but the humor was lost on her.

Victor continued: "San Pedro will be known for more than just a port and factories. It's going to be a modern hub for food, arts and culture…and no crazy dog was going to keep me from seeing that through. To my best friend of fifteen years, my son who inspires me more and more each day to be a better man and to Lucy, a girl who has managed to charm my Martin, let's cheers to possibilities."

After the celebratory tapping of glasses, Victor brought the glass to his lips and took a sip. He lowered his glass some, closed his eyes and savored the wine. Lucy and Martin continued to drink, while Jim spooned potato salad onto his plate.

"It's probably best to dig in," Jim said, "mister wine connoisseur here is going to be a while."

"It should be savored," Victor said, "you don't guzzle a fifty-year-old merlot."

Martin and Lucy started to scoop the food onto their plates when the doorbell rang.

"Are you expecting someone?" Jim asked.

"No."

"I'll get it," Jim said.

Jim walked to the door. Lucy watched through the sliding glass as the door opened. She was afraid it was Garza coming to check on things, and assuming his usual front as a gardener looking for new business in rich neighborhoods.

Instead, a man entered the house dressed in a light blue UCLA T-shirt and jeans. He was holding a large roll of sheet paper. He seemed familiar, but Lucy struggled to place him. Jim led the man onto the patio and the man greeted them, and then introduced himself to Lucy.

"Taylor Barnes," he said as he shook Lucy's hand.

"You just missed the toast," Victor said.

"I got hung up with some contractors. I've brought the new plans," Taylor said.

"Thanks. You can sit them over there." Victor pointed to a wicker table and Taylor dropped the plans on it.

"This looks great," Taylor said as he pulled a chair from the table and prepared to sit. "What's the story on the wine? Please tell me it's a Merlot."

"Sure is. Courtesy of our guest, Lucy."

"It smells divine," Taylor said."

"Lucy, here, knows a wine enthusiast. You'd want to get on her good side if you're looking to snag a few rare bottles."

"It's a small collection, really, "Lucy said, "I doubt there would be much there of interest."

"You never know," Taylor said, "I read an article about a man who had held on to a couple of bottles passed down by his father. Little did he know three of those bottles would fetch him about two million. Your friend could be sitting on a gold mine."

"I'll pass that info along to him," Lucy said as she took a bite of potato salad.

"Go ahead, Taylor, you can have my glass," Victor said. "I'm still taking these pain-killers and I probably shouldn't be drinking."

Taylor didn't hesitate. He picked up the glass and took a sip, paused and then took another. Lucy watched silently but inside she felt like she was drowning. The poison appeared to have no effect on Victor, but given the amount of wine Taylor was consuming, soon he would be the one collapsing. He prepared to take another sip when Lucy intervened: "How about I get you a fresh glass," she said.

Taylor looked at her confused but reluctantly gave her the glass.

"This bottle is supposed to be served chilled. It's been sitting and has probably warmed up."

Taylor perked up at the idea. "That sounds lovely, Lucy."

Lucy took the poisoned glass to the kitchen. She emptied the wine into the sink and rinsed the glass with water. She tried to imagine what Garza would say about her failed attempt—then she realized he wouldn't say anything, he would act. It was that action that she feared.

Lucy returned to the table with untainted wine and served it to Taylor.

"It packs quite the punch doesn't it," he said. His face was drained ashen and a blotchy discoloring had formed around his neck.

"Are you all right?" Victor asked.

"I don't know. I'm feeling a little hot."

"Get him some water."

Martin rushed to the kitchen, poured a glass of water and quickly brought it to Taylor. He urged him to drink but Taylor couldn't keep the water down. He heaved violently and spewed the water onto the table.

"I'll call 911," Lucy said.

"Use the phone in the kitchen so they know the address," Victor said.

She went into the house and found the phone on the hutch, buried underneath bills and magazines. She hesitated for a moment and considered letting Taylor die—after all, an ambulance and the possibility of police was the greatest danger she and Garza faced. But Taylor was an inconvenience, and his death would signify nothing. Lucy dialed 911 and when the operator answered, she said: "Come now. There's a man—he's having a heart-attack or something… hurry!"

She watched from the kitchen, as all three men tended to Taylor. The water spewing from his mouth had turned red, and Lucy remembered what she had read online about the poison. Internal bleeding was the second stage. There would be three stages in all, with the last being cardiac arrest. She watched the men change, each one penetrated by fear, realizing their friend was dying. They were reduced to helpless figures moving about in horror. At least someone close to Victor would die, and that would have to do for now. She took the half-emptied bottle and left the house. Once outside, she ran to where Garza had parked.

As she moved closer to the van, Garza started the engine. She nearly dropped the bottle as she cut across the lawn. Martin appeared sprinting behind her. He was closing the distance. Garza gestured for Lucy to run faster. Realizing

Martin was close enough to grab her, Garza got out of the van with his pistol. Lucy reached for the van's passenger door and Martin took hold of her arm.

"What the hell is going on?" Martin asked as he spun her around. "What did you do?"

Lucy couldn't speak. Garza held the pistol on Martin and he released Lucy's arm. Lucy got into the van and Garza opened the rear door.

"Inside," Garza demanded of Martin.

"Who the hell are you?"

"Don't make me shoot you, boy. Do as I say!"

Sirens blared in the distance. Garza was growing impatient. He needed the boy alive, but he also needed him afraid. He pulled the hammer back and shoved the gun into Martin's ribs.

"Shit, man," Martin said as he climbed into the back of the van. "What is this, Lucy? What's going on? Answer me, please. I don't understand."

Garza struck the boy in the back of the head with the pistol's butt and locked the van doors. He got back inside and drove away, passing the ambulance as it entered the affluent enclave.

CHAPTER ELEVEN

THE VAN WAS PARKED in Garza's garage. Martin was in the back, his head bleeding where Garza had struck him, and he was pleading for his life. His cries fell on deaf ears. As much as Lucy wanted to tell him that he'd be all right, she couldn't muster the lie. Garza had used Sarge's chain, fastening it to metal hooks in the van and wrapping it around Martin's ankles. He used rope to bind his wrists behind his back.

"Why are you doing this?" Martin cried. "What is it you want from me?"

"Shut up," Garza said, "keep talking and I'll gag you."

"He'll come for me."

"Your father?"

"He's not going to wait for the police," Martin said, "he's going to find you."

Garza took a pair of garden shears from a small box and walked over to Martin. He placed his hand over Martin's mouth and cut a half inch of flesh from his ear. Even though Martin's scream was muffled, it resonated in the garage.

Paco barked and howled from the commotion, yanking

at his chain as if excited by the violence being carried out a few feet away from him.

The shears were sharp and the cut clean. Garza exhibited the piece of ear in front Martin causing him to lose consciousness. He wrapped the flesh in a rag and went into the house. Lucy was standing at the doorway leading to the kitchen, horrified—tears streamed down her face.

"Did you really have to do that?" she asked.

"Yes. He needs to know we were serious."

"Pulling a gun on him wasn't enough?"

"No, it wasn't."

"And what if his father doesn't come?"

"He'll come," Garza said as he rinsed the piece of ear in the sink.

"I'm going to see about him," Lucy said, "I don't want his ear to get infected."

"That's the least of his worries but go ahead."

Garza gave the piece of ear to Lucy.

"What am I supposed to do with this?" she asked.

"Take pictures with the boy's phone. Then send them to Victor."

Garza washed his hands and poured a glass of whiskey before heading to the sofa to watch television.

Lucy applied ointment she found in the bathroom cabinet. She bandaged Martin's ear with gauze. Martin was still passed out. He woke after thirty minutes, disoriented. His mouth was dry, and his face was swollen. He stared at Lucy in agony; she was forced to look away. She felt sick and knew it was only going to get worse for Martin.

"Please help me," he said.

"I can't."

"Why are you doing this? I don't understand."

"It's not you, Martin. This is about your father."

"My father? But he adores you. It's the old man, isn't it? He's making you do this?"

"No, he's not," Lucy said calmly as she dabbed the remainder of blood from his ear with cotton.

"He isn't your grandfather, is he?"

"No. He's nobody…just a man who is helping me."

"It's something my father did?" Martin asked.

"Yes."

"To you? Did he hurt you?"

"He hurt someone I loved. Your father isn't who you think he is."

"I'm sorry for whatever he did, Lucy. I truly am but this isn't right. My fucking ear, Lucy? This guy is insane. I know this isn't you. I know it!"

"I'm sorry, Martin. I have to do this."

"Lucy, the cops will kill you. Think about what you're doing!"

"Yes, I know. I've considered that."

"Lucy, we have to get out of here. Just let me go—we can go to together."

"I wish I could. I really do."

"Let me fucking go, Lucy!"

Lucy could hear Garza coming from the kitchen. "I'm sorry, Martin." Lucy picked up the garden shears, then put them to Martin's throat. "You're going to call your father now," she said.

Garza handed Lucy a piece of paper. Written on the paper was what Martin was to tell his father on the phone—it was instructions on where to meet them.

"Where is this?" she whispered.

Garza pulled her away from Martin and she removed the shears from his throat. They talked softly.

"A warehouse near the port," Garza said, "Victor will go

135

there and wait for further instructions. He's to come alone. If he doesn't—we'll kill the boy."

"We aren't really going to kill him, are we? None of this is his fault and we've already taken half his ear."

Garza looked at Lucy, intensely. "That's not our choice. It's his father's—if he wants his son to live, he'll follow our instructions. You make sure he understands that."

Lucy sighed. "Okay."

Garza went back into the house and left Lucy to tend to Martin.

"That man is going to kill you if you don't do what I say, Martin. Do you understand?" Lucy asked softly.

Martin nodded. He was tired and had loss significant blood.

"We're going to take you to your father. If you do what we say, you're going to make it through this."

"I would never have imagined this—"

"What?"

"You trying to kill me. I guess that's what love gets you these days?"

"You don't know what you're saying. You don't love me—you couldn't possibly."

"It's the only thing I'm sure of—pretty fucked up, huh?"

"You're in shock. I need your phone."

Martin handed Lucy his phone and she dialed Victor from his contact list. She made sure the speaker was on.

"Martin? Are you okay?" Victor asked; he was frantic.

"Dad, I'm okay."

"Is it money? Is that what they want?"

"No."

"Did they hurt you?"

"You need to listen to me dad."

"Okay."

"They want to meet but there can't be anyone else, no police, not even Jim. You understand?"

Victor hesitated. "I got it."

"When the time comes, they will call you and tell you where to meet. That is where they will make trade."

"The trade?" Victor asked.

"My life for yours, dad."

Lucy ended the call. To emphasize the point, Lucy texted Victor pictures of Martin's mangled ear. Afterwards, she destroyed the phone, smashing it with Garza's 16 once hammer and soaking it in bleach.

Lucy sat with Martin in the back of the van. The night had turned cool and the air was still, even Paco had quieted. She wanted to let Martin go but knew there was no other way to get Victor to show up at the warehouse. Using Martin was the only plan she thought still had a good chance of working but then again, she hadn't been thinking too clearly. She tried to retrace her steps to pinpoint when everything had gone wrong. Maybe if she had never gone to Martin's job, he wouldn't have gotten involved? She sucked him into the chaos and now he was lying in a van missing half of an ear. Garza had warned Lucy to stay away from Martin and she didn't listen. Why was she so drawn to him? Was it love?

"Taylor is dead, isn't he?" Martin asked.

"I think so," Lucy replied in a shattered voice. "I don't see how he could have lived."

"It was in the wine wasn't it—poison?"

"Yes."

"Meant for my dad?"

"Yes."

"How do you know the old man won't kill us both?"

"He isn't going to kill us. We have an arrangement."

"What makes you so sure? Look at him. There's nothing

in his eyes—I mean he's empty."

"And how do you know so much?" Lucy asked. "You don't even know what your own father is capable of."

"Then spill it. What is this all about, Lucy? I think you owe me at least that."

"You wouldn't believe me. I've seen how you look at him. He's everything to you and I'm just—"

"You're just what?"

Lucy struggled to get the words out. "Soto…he did something to my mother."

"What the hell does that mean?"

"He hurt her."

"You're going to have to be clearer than that."

"I can't—not with you."

"If you're worried about hurting me, that moment has passed. Now you look me in the face and tell me. Say it, damn you! You owe me at least that. Tell me why I'm here!"

"Victor killed my mother! I don't know how or why, but she died because him."

Martin was silent. He stared at Lucy as if he were in a trance. It was an icy glare reminiscent of the looks Garza had given her.

"Say something," Lucy said.

Martin closed his eyes and rested his head against the wall of the van. Lucy went into the house unsure of the damage she had done.

CHAPTER TWELVE

LUCY GOT A MERE FOUR HOURS of sleep while Garza slept soundly in his room. Lucy couldn't stop thinking about Martin and she periodically checked on him throughout the night. When she encountered him awake, he'd close his eyes as if to wish her away. He never once tried to escape or reason with her to set him free, and Lucy didn't know what to make of his passiveness. What was going through his mind? Had Martin come to terms with his predicament? It was feasible Victor wouldn't play by Garza's rules, and perhaps in Martin's solitude he considered his father's arrogance could get him killed. Or had he truly considered what Lucy had told him—that his father was a murderer? The emptiness in Martin's eyes gave no indication of the thoughts lurking inside his head, and Lucy found this more unsettling than when he said he loved her.

• • •

The sun broke over the fence in the backyard. Paco stirred with hunger. Lucy fed the dog three biscuits and gave him fresh water. Martin sat quietly in the van with his legs pulled into his chest watching Lucy tend to Paco.

"That dog gets treated better than me," Martin said snidely.

Lucy piped up: "I can make you breakfast—whatever you want."

"I've been thinking all night—didn't sleep for shit."

"Sorry."

"No, you're not," Martin said.

"I already told you, Martin. It was never about you. It's always been about Victor."

"Yes. My father. I know."

"I didn't want to hurt you," Lucy said, "I need you to know that."

Lucy looked away from Martin. A tear was threating to slip from her left eye and her voice was beginning to crack.

"I want to believe that—I do," Martin said, "but in a few hours, I may be dead."

Lucy didn't know how to respond. She knew he was right, that their conversation could soon be obsolete, and a thought echoed, endlessly—what if Garza kills Martin? Taylor was surely dead, though Lucy felt little remorse. But Martin was different, Lucy couldn't fathom having his blood on her hands. The idea gave her a shiver and when she couldn't bear to consider it any longer, she went into the kitchen to scramble eggs for Martin's breakfast.

Martin was grateful when Lucy brought the food to him. He spooned the eggs quickly into his mouth. When Martin asked for something to drink, Lucy brought him one of Garza's beers—it was all they had aside from liquor, coffee, and water from the tap. Lucy thought the beer would help Martin relax. She watched him guzzle it fast. When he finished, he gave an exhausted sigh and stared at her with the same coldness as before. Lucy knew no matter what was to come, that part of Martin was already ruined by the whole ordeal. A person couldn't come back from having a chunk of their ear cut off with shears. It was the type of malevolence that stained their consciousness so deep that even the best therapy wouldn't be able to scrub it away.

Garza announced from the living room that they would be leaving soon and ordered Lucy to ready Paco. Lucy left Martin alone so she could tend to the dog, who had long finished the biscuits and was circling the yard. She fastened the leash to Paco's body harness. The dog was already worked up, it was as if he knew what was coming—like Sarge before him, it would be Paco's time to prove his usefulness.

Garza appeared dressed in black work pants, boots, and a long coat. He wore a knit cap on his head and a pair of leather gloves were shoved into his coat pocket. Lucy knew his revolver was holstered somewhere on his body and he was sure to be carrying extra bullets. He rummaged around in the corner of the garage and then pulled a small machine from a box.

"What's that?" Lucy asked.

"A pressure washer—we'll need to clean up after ourselves."

Lucy wanted to be sick but fought back the urge.

"The dog will ride up front with us," Garza said, "make sure the boy is tied up good. We can't risk him getting loose."

"I understand," Lucy said.

"There's a pay phone near the port. Call Victor and tell him we will be meeting at Warehouse 50, at the farthest end of the berths."

"After we're in the warehouse, what do we do then?"

"We'll keep Martin tied up and lay him out on the warehouse floor. Paco will keep watch over him. When Victor arrives, you'll let him in. He'll see Martin is still alive, then we exchange Victor for Martin. We throw Victor in the back of the van with Paco and we drive the hell out of there."

"What about Martin?"

"I told you, he isn't our concern."

"We can't just leave him in the warehouse. Who will know to look for him?"

"You can send him a cab."

Lucy scoffed at the idea. "And Victor—what do we do with his body?"

Lucy hung on Garza's every word, watching the scenes unfold in her mind.

"You get the answers you need from him and when you're satisfied, you kill him. We light the van on fire with him in the back. You pay me what you owe me, and we disappear—go our separate ways—or you come work for me."

"Work for you?" Lucy asked.

"I've been giving it some thought. I think we make a good team."

Lucy didn't respond. She didn't want to upset Garza but the thought of working with him—killing people—made her want to vomit.

"You don't have to decide now but give it some consideration. There's a lot I could teach you. You've got a real knack for this work."

"I do?"

"Sure, you're smart and with practice you could be one of the best."

It was high-praise coming from Garza. No one had ever said Lucy was good at anything before.

"Let's just get though today," Lucy said.

Driving to the meeting place, Lucy's thoughts were racing. The word *freedom* was bouncing about in her brain like the white numbered balls churning in a lottery machine. She wrestled with the idea that she had been carrying out vengeance in the name of freedom, believing that killing Victor Soto would release the shackles that had kept her bound for so long, and light could finally pierce the dark clouds that had remained after her mother's murder. But the sickening truth was that Lucy had never felt more like a prisoner. Justice for her mother was the thing she wanted most, but she had long forgotten the nuances and tangibles she once clung to—her mother's scent, her walk and touch—what if vengeance wasn't the road to rectitude, but the curse of more impenetrable darkness? The memory of her mother had grown distorted over time and when she thought of her, it was no longer a feeling of melancholy and longing but of hate—deep and painful. Lucy hated that her mother left her alone and she hated that Victor had gotten away with killing her; but what Lucy hated most was the notion that her mother, so desperate to ascend from poverty, felt it necessary to carry on with a vile man like Victor Soto, and now, here Lucy was, becoming a murderer like him.

The van rumbled down Gaffey Street, Lucy with Paco between her and Garza, and the assaulted Martin sliding about in the back. With each thud Martin released a deep moan followed by a string of curses. Lucy did her best to keep Paco from moving, but Paco hadn't spent much time in the van and the motion seemed to make him nervous.

As the van approached the port, Lucy could see ships in the horizon. Garza made a series of turns and parked down a dirt road with a pay phone, one of the last few in San Pedro. He handed Lucy a quarter and she got out of the van. She had copied Victor's phone number from Martin's contact list on a piece of paper. She took the paper from her pocket and called Victor.

"Hello?" Victor said. He was frantic and there was fear in his voice.

Lucy spoke measured but deliberate: "Warehouse 50. San Pedro. Come now." Lucy hung up the phone and got back into the van.

The warm wind rattled the windows of the van as Garza made the steady approach toward the berths. The warehouses were in the oldest part of Ports O' Call, half a mile away from the shops, restaurants, and tourists. It was desolate real estate that Soto's development team had been so intent on turning into million-dollar waterfront property—sky-rises, boutique hotels and shops, yet it all would amount to nothing more than sketches and blueprints. There would be no development, no up-sale to the yuppies and hipsters because that dream would die with Soto.

Lucy was flush and sweating as they approached Warehouse 50. Her nerves were shot, and she couldn't shake the feeling something wasn't right. She stared out the window intently, but nothing looked out of the ordinary. What was ordinary for the berths? Aside from the scattered steel beams, burnt and rusted shipping crates, and graffitied aluminum sheeting?

Garza parked in front of the warehouse. It appeared to be abandoned. The lock on the doors had long been removed indicating there was nothing inside worth stealing. Garza stepped out of the van with his hand on his pistol. The old man surveyed the landscape and when he was satisfied, he opened the van's passenger-side door, took Paco by the leash, and led him out of the van. Garza was familiar with Warehouse 50—he had used the location many times in the past. It was far away from shoppers at the port and nearest apartment was two-miles away. A man could scream and plead, and the ocean would swallow up the noise. It was a decent kill house and when it was all over, he could wash down the blood and bits from the concrete floor with the pressure washer.

Lucy stayed in the van and watched as Paco led the old man into the warehouse.

"What's happening?" Martin asked.

"Relax—you'll be safe soon," Lucy replied, "as long as your father does as he's told."

Garza appeared from the building and summoned to Lucy to let Martin out. Lucy got out of the van and moved to its rear. She opened the doors and Martin shuffled forward as if desperate to feel the sun on his face. He looked to the sky, basking in the warmth for a moment, and then he completely emerged from the van's rear. Lucy worked to keep him steady, leading him into the warehouse.

"What is this place?" Martin asked.

"Just move," Lucy said as Paco walked beside them.

When they entered the warehouse, Garza had found a folding chair and had placed it in the middle of the building's floor. The warehouse smelled of fish and salt—likely a commercial fishermen's hub for sorting their catch. Bird droppings and white dust covered the concrete floor, and the same metal beams stacked outside, lined the warehouse walls.

Garza retrieved the rope from the van. When he returned, he ordered Lucy to tie Martin to the chair.

"Quickly," he said, "Soto will be arriving soon."

Lucy helped Martin to the chair and proceeded to tie his ankles and wrists. She took additional pieces of rope and wrapped them around his torso. Martin didn't protest—he seemed docile, accepting even.

Garza watched for cars from a warehouse window. There was nothing but an eerie quiet. Then, Garza spotted something off in the distance. As it moved closer, he recognized it as a black SUV, hulking and American. There were no vehicles trailing it. Garza sighed a little relief; he had been prepared to kill Martin the moment he saw a convoy and the lone SUV let him know Soto wasn't a total fool—but it didn't mean that Soto wouldn't try something else, something stupid. Garza needed Martin alive long enough to make the swap, but he was no fool. Martin was and would always be a loose end and Garza knew he would have to find a way to kill him.

"A truck is coming," Garza announced. Lucy was holding Paco's leash and watching over the restrained Martin.

"Your father better not do anything dumb for your sake," Lucy said.

"He won't," Martin said.

"How do you know?"

"I know my father. I'm all he has now. He won't put me in danger."

"Okay."

"But once I'm safe…he'll kill you and the old man."

"What?"

"I know the type of man my father was. I know he deserves this but he's always one step ahead. You and the old man aren't going to make it out of this alive."

The SUV parked in front of the warehouse. For a moment, no one got out—Garza tapped his foot, counting the seconds until someone appeared. Then, a door opened, and Soto exited slowly. He walked with the aid of one crutch and seemed to struggle just to remain upright. He was dressed in a black suit and dark tie and looked as if he had come from a funeral. Soto approached the warehouse door. Garza raised his gun and opened the door enough to see Soto limping toward him.

"Right there is good," Garza shouted through the crack in

the door. "And put your hands up so I can see them."

"I'll fall. I need the crutch."

Soto used his right hand to brace himself with the crutch and raised his left.

"Anyone else in that truck?" Garza asked.

"No. I came alone like you said. Now let me see my son."

"Take off your clothes," Garza said.

"What?"

"You heard me. Take them off."

"What the hell for?"

"You want to see your boy again or not? Now take off your fucking clothes."

Soto leaned against the SUV, using it to steady himself as he began to remove his clothing, one article at a time. First, he took off his suit coat, then his tie and shirt, followed by his shoes and finally his pants. When he was down to his briefs and socks, Garza opened the door to the warehouse and let him in. He looked hard at the SUV, searching for any indication someone else was inside. He wanted to search the truck thoroughly, but he couldn't risk leaving Soto alone with Lucy. Even with Paco by her side, Soto could have the upper-hand.

Soto limped toward Martin, "You all right, son?" he asked.

Martin nodded but said nothing.

"You are fucking animals," Soto said, "you have no idea what you've done."

"Careful or I'll cripple you for good," Garza said.

"Well, you got me here. Now is someone going to tell me what this is about? How about you?" Soto said, looking to Lucy. "You're quite the conniving bitch. What kind of trick did you play on my son to get him to bring you to our home? I'm guessing you spiked Taylor's wine, too and put him in a fucking coma."

Lucy gave a look of surprise upon hearing Taylor had survived.

"Well speak, damn you!" Soto demanded.

Garza pressed the gun barrel to Soto's head and whispered softly, "You're not in charge. This isn't your fucking office. We will ask the questions and you will answer. Otherwise that dog takes a bite out of your son and then a bite out of you. Understood?"

"All right," Soto said. "Whatever."

"Good," Garza said, "now she's going to ask you some questions. You answer honestly, and you get to keep your balls. You lie and I let the dog loose."

Lucy began: "Before we met, Victor, I knew you—I knew your voice. I was a little girl when I first heard it. You spoke to me from my mother's cell phone."

"I don't know what you're talking about."

"Her name was Rita. She was beautiful—long black hair, hazel eyes, and when she would walk into rooms men like you turned to putty."

"I don't know any Rita—never have."

Garza struck Soto with the butt of the gun hard enough to sting.

"What the hell!" Soto cried.

"I told you not to lie. Next time it's the dog," Garza said.

Lucy continued: "You were on the phone that night, Victor. You were panicked because you had done something—something terrible, and then you hung up. Did you ever think about the little girl on the other end? Did I ever cross your mind? She was all I had, and you took her away from me and I want to know why."

Soto stared at his son. Martin was expressionless, as if to cope with the trauma his cognizance had evacuated. And Soto's face was no longer that of an A.D.A. with lofty ambitions, but rather that of a father stripped bare in front of his son, being forced to reveal what he had hidden for over a decade. It was an attrition of Soto's soul, and the only chance of keeping his son alive was to unburden himself.

"Just tell them, Dad," Martin finally said, "tell her what she wants to know, and it will be over."

"Martin? You don't understand, son."

"It's okay, Dad. I know you were different back then—I know the type of man you really are. You're a good man. I know that. and Mom knew that, too."

Soto was quiet for a moment—he could hardly look Lucy in the eyes.

"Rita has haunted me in more ways than I'd ever imagine. We met at a party for Judge Swenson. He was the judge I was clerking for at the time and she was beautiful. I fell for her instantly and over a few months we started seeing each other, regularly. Then months became years and whatever little time I had, I spent with her. And the day came for me to graduate law school, and to celebrate we went away to Catalina. It was one of the best times of my life. I loved Rita, you understand?"

"Bullshit," Lucy said.

"You have to understand that we came from two different worlds—and it would have never worked out between us."

"When exactly did you decide to kill her?"

"I'm no killer! I told her we couldn't be together and that it was best to end things. For years we didn't see each other. She went her way and I went mine. But she'd call from time to time asking for money..."

"Fuck you, man!" Lucy shouted. "My mother never asked anyone for shit."

Lucy released slack from Paco's leash and the dog charged at Soto.

"It's the truth," Soto said.

"My mother wasn't some cling-on looking for handouts."

Paco lunged and growled at Soto's feet. Lucy used all her strength to keep him under control.

"Your mother was a survivor and I respected her for it. Still, I had moved on and was going to start a family. But she knew things about me, things that I had told her in confidence. She threatened to make information public and I needed to be vetted by the city. She wanted money to keep quiet. I agreed to see her one last time."

"I think he's stalling for his cop buddies," Garza said.

"No one is coming," Soto said, "I'm telling you the truth."

"I know a liar when I see one," Garza pointed his pistol at Soto.

"I didn't kill Rita. I rejected her, and she took it hard. She probably went back to using, and for all I know that's what she wanted the money for."

"My mother gave up drugs for good before I was born. She would never have asked you for shit unless…"

"I'm sorry but maybe you didn't know her like you thought you did," Victor said.

Lucy moved closer to Soto. Paco was at her side and growing more aggressive. "It makes sense now. I should have seen it. All these years, I never considered it. How could I have not put it together?"

The color was beginning to drain from Soto's face and his body had succumbed to a slight tremor as he continued to balance himself with the crutch. Lucy and Paco circled Soto. She took deliberate steps, looking at his body, pausing to focus on his shoulders, back, legs, and then finally stopping at his left side.

Soto watched the dog intently. Each time Paco moved, he flinched and drew back.

Lucy inspected a patch of pale, dry skin on the side of Soto's stomach. Then she lifted her shirt to expose the similar patches on her stomach. Their patches were distinctly identical, rough white skin, scaled and flaky. Soto watched in horror.

"The doctor called it genodermatoses—said it was a genetic skin condition passed on by a parent. It was just another fucking thing I had to deal with as a kid—being too self-conscience to swim in a pool because kids would say I had the plague. My mother didn't have it, so I knew it had to be from my father—whoever the fuck he was."

"It can't be," Soto said, "she had an abortion. I drove her myself."

"She was Catholic, Victor. And I was her second chance."

Lucy looked to Martin whose tears flowed into his lap. Her knees buckled—she struggled to breathe. It was as if the air had thinned and with each breath, her lungs felt more useless. She was losing her grip on Paco's leash.

"Martin, I'm so sorry—I'm so sorry," Soto cried.

"It can't be…we can't be," Martin said.

"Oh God!" Soto pleaded. "What have I done?"

Martin's lower lip trembled. Soto fell beside him and threw his arms around his shoulders. The bound Martin tried to pull away and began screaming at his father.

Garza took the leash from Lucy's grip and led Paco away from the chaos that was unfolding. "Clock is ticking," Garza said as he extended the pistol for Lucy to take.

Lucy grabbed the pistol from Garza's hand and put it to Soto's head.

Soto clung to Martin. "Please, it's enough now—don't you see that we all have suffered."

"But you haven't suffered, Victor. Not like me," Lucy said as she cocked the pistol's hammer. She could barely hold the gun steady.

"Do it Lucita and be done with it," Garza said.

"Tell me, damnit!" Lucy demanded. "How did my mother die?"

"Okay, okay. We were arguing. I tried to reason with her. I just wanted her to listen but there was no convincing her—she was going to the press. I hit her and I didn't stop—I couldn't stop. It was like I wasn't in control. There was blood and then I didn't recognize her anymore. The phone rang, and it was you."

"And your cop pal, Jim, helped cover it up?" Lucy asked.

"He said no one would miss her."

"Well, she was missed, damn you!" Lucy's finger was pressed firmly on the trigger when Paco began to bark, looking upward toward the rafters. Three shots echoed through the structure. A bullet pierced Lucy's arm sending her to the floor. Another shot narrowly missed Garza. Paco broke free from Garza and ran. It was as if he could taste freedom; he made his way to the opening of the warehouse doors and forced his body through to the other side—Paco was gone.

Lucy looked in the direction of the gun fire. Jim was crouched down in the warehouse's ceiling rafters with his scoped rifle pointed at her. Lucy sought cover, thinking how foolish it was not to have searched the SUV. Had Jim been in the truck the whole time? Or had he followed in another car, parking and then closing in on the warehouse by foot?

Jim had climbed to the rafters from the outside and through the window with the aid of the stacked beams. He had a high-powered rifle and had set-up with a good view of the entire warehouse. Lucy knew they had to get to the van, or they were surely dead.

"The gun! Give me the gun," Garza shouted.

Lucy slid the gun to Garza. He aimed and fired at Jim

while Lucy rushed to Martin's aid. She quickly untied Martin. Martin stood for a moment, and then looked back at his father who was lying on the warehouse floor.

Martin took Lucy's hand. "We have to get out of here," she said.

"We need to get to the van," Garza shouted to Lucy.

Jim continued to fire at Garza, ignoring Lucy whose proximity to Martin likely kept Jim from training his rifle on her.

Lucy and Martin ran toward the exit. Soto had cowered into a corner away from the gunfire.

Lucy and Martin exited the warehouse. Garza continued to fire at Jim. As Garza reached the warehouse door, he turned and fired at Soto but missed.

"Paco?" Lucy asked.

"He took off." Garza replied.

"Where do we go now?" Lucy asked.

"Far away from here," Garza said, "we need miles between us and San Pedro."

Garza shot out the tires of Soto's SUV.

Lucy helped Martin into the van with Garza behind the wheel. Lucy tended to her wound the best she could, applying pressure but the blood persisted.

"How bad is it?" Garza asked.

"I think the bullet went clean through."

"What are you planning to do with the kid?"

"He's with us."

"He's a liability," Garza said.

"I said he's with us."

"Where we headed?"

"My apartment," Lucy said, "My arm…it needs attention. I can treat it there. Head downtown."

Garza merged onto the 110 North from Gaffey Street towards downtown. As the van gained speed, it rode into the sea of cars flowing toward the smog swamped buildings in the distance.

CHAPTER THIRTEEN

WHEN THEY ARRIVED at Lucy's apartment, Garza parked the van in an alleyway that was overrun with brush and garbage. Inside the apartment, Martin stood quietly as Garza sutured Lucy's wound with a hot bobby pin and waxed dental floss. She bit her lip through the process; Martin moved closer and took her hand. Thinking about the intimacy she and Martin shared had pressed her psyche in a way that made her wish for a lobotomy. If her mind wasn't focused on keeping free of the cops, she would have given into every screaming impulse to succumb to madness—to completely check out. Each time she looked at Martin, she felt the harsh sting of shame and guilt. She knew Martin was crumbling inside. There was something in his eyes—his tenderness and innocence had been excavated leaving behind something fragmented.

When Garza finished sewing her arm, he applied rubbing alcohol and antibiotic cream that was more than a year old. It was all Lucy could find and it was better than nothing.

"Now what?" Lucy asked.

Garza sighed, looking out the window. "We need to leave."

"And Martin?"

Garza was silent.

"I think I should go with you," Martin said.

"What the hell is wrong with you? You aren't thinking straight? I tried to kill Victor—fuck, our father."

"I can't go back—not now—not knowing what I know."

"Your life is here."

"What life?" Martin snapped. "Everything has changed—there's no going back."

"How can you even look at me?" Lucy asked avoiding Martin's watery stare.

Garza interrupted: "The police will come for him. He's a hostage as far as they know."

There was a hard knock on the door. Garza's hand shot to his pistol and both Martin and Lucy moved toward the corner of the room. There was another knock—harder.

"The police?" Lucy asked.

Garza took a few steps toward the door with his pistol raised.

"Lucy!" A voice shouted. "I know you're in there. I can hear you. Open the damn door."

"Who is that?" Garza asked.

"It's Kip," Lucy said.

"Who the fuck is Kip?"

"Just some guy. I can get rid of him," Lucy said.

"Do it," Garza instructed. "We don't have time for this shit."

"What do you want?" Lucy shouted through the door.

"I want to talk. I know you're in trouble."

"What are you talking about?"

"It's all on the news. Your picture along with the old guy's."

"Fuck!" Lucy said looking to Garza, helplessly. "What the hell do we do now?"

Garza moved closer toward the door and looked through the peep hole. "He's alone. Go ahead and let him in."

"You sure we should do that?" Lucy asked.

"Let him in," Garza repeated.

Lucy unlocked the door and opened it slowly. Kip pushed his way in.

"What the hell?" Lucy cried.

"I knew you were nuts but shit!" Kip said. "You really are fucking out there…"

Kip came to a halt mid-sentence as he stared at the tip of Garza's pistol.

"Wait, wait. I'm sorry," Kip said.

"Sit down," Garza demanded.

Kip took a seat on the bed. Martin cowered in the corner and Lucy stood over Kip with her fist balled tight.

"Please don't hurt me," Kip cried.

"No one's going to hurt you. What's this about us on the news?" Lucy asked.

"It's everywhere. They're saying you kidnapped some important guy's son and tried to kill him—some are even calling you terrorists."

"Terrorists?" Garza said, "how the fuck did we become terrorists?"

"You talk to anyone? You tell anyone about me or that I live here?" Lucy asked.

"No. I didn't say a word," Kip said. "I came straight here when I saw it on the news at the gym."

"Why are you here?" Garza asked.

"I wanted to see if Lucy was all right."

"Bullshit."

"He knows when you're lying so it's better to come out with it," Lucy said.

Kip looked to Martin. Then he looked to Garza who kept

a firm grip on his pistol and a stone-faced expression.

"I came to talk," Kip said.

"About what?" Lucy asked.

"About how we could help each other."

"You want to help us?"

"Yeah. Why not?"

"Maybe because I told you I never wanted to see you again?"

"I thought you may have had a change of heart."

"I don't have time for this."

"I can get you out of town," Kip said.

"How?" Lucy asked.

"I have a friend—a client with a boat in Marina Del Rey. I know where she keeps the keys. You can take it down to Mexico."

"What's in it for you?"

"I need some cash."

"Cash?" Lucy asked. "What makes you think I have cash to give you?"

"I've seen your banking statements lying around."

"That money is gone. I withdrew it."

"All of it?" Kip asked.

"Most of it…maybe a grand is left."

"That's fine," Kip said pipping up. "I'll take whatever you have, and the boat is yours."

"How do you expect us to get to the marina?" Lucy asked.

"You can take my car," Kip said.

"I thought you drove a motorcycle?" Lucy asked.

"Not always—I've got a hybrid. They won't be looking for you in my car." Kip pulled the keys from his pocket and held them up for Garza and Lucy to inspect.

"How do we know we can even trust this guy?" Garza asked.

"You can trust me—Lucy knows I got her back."

"That so Lucy?" Garza asked.

Lucy paused for a moment and then answered: "It's the only chance we have of getting out of here."

"Mexico? The authorities will be looking for us at every point of entry," Martin said.

"I know a few ways in. I have contacts there that could help us," Garza said.

"All right," Lucy said. "I'll get the money out of the ATM on the way to the marina."

Kip smiled and stood up, his gym shorts a size too big hung baggily and swayed.

"What is that?" Garza asked Kip.

"What is what?" Kip asked.

"In your pocket…take it out."

"It's my phone."

"I said take it out!"

Garza stood with the pistol pointed at Kip's head.

"It's just a phone, man. What's the big deal?"

"Kip just take it out of your pocket," Lucy said.

A look of panic washed over Kip's face, followed by help-lessness. He reached into this pocket slowly and took out the phone. He displayed it for Lucy to see—the screen exhibited a current call to 911. The line had been in use for approximately fifteen minutes and counting.

"What the hell?" Lucy said.

"They're talking about a reward…ten thousand for infor-mation. I figured if I turned you guys over, I might get some old charges dropped and the cash—win, win."

Garza quickly put the pistol to Kip's head and pulled the trigger. Blood and brain tissue sprayed across the tie-dyed tapestry hanging over Lucy's bed.

Martin turned to face the wall, unable to look at Kip's body as the blood poured from the wound. Lucy stood frozen listening as the dispatcher on the other end of the cell phone shouted desperately for Kip. The dispatcher announced help would arrive soon before disconnecting.

"We're getting out of here," Garza said lowering the pistol.

Lucy was frantic—there was panic in her voice. "You didn't have to kill him."

"The police will be here soon," Garza said, calmly.

"I can't go with you," Martin said, "I don't know what I'm going to do but I can't go with you."

"He's going to talk to the cops," Garza said.

"Martin?" Lucy asked. Her voice was gentle as she reached out to touch his shoulder. Martin pulled away.

"I won't say anything about you, so you don't have to worry."

"You're standing in a room with a dead man. You don't have a choice. You will talk. You're going to tell them everything," Garza said as he approached Martin.

Martin began to quiver. Garza gripped his shoulder. He stared into Martin's eyes with a depth and visceral knowing. Martin fought to lower his head and escape Garza's stare, but Garza forced his chin upright with his fist. Martin sunk into a desolate weep.

"It's okay—it's okay," Garza said. "You are who you are. We are who we are. We should have never crossed paths—it should have never happened."

Tears flowed as Martin nodded his head in agreement. Lucy looked on, unable to move—it was a side of Garza she had never seen before. He was tender and it made her chest grow tight with unease. Garza was a cunning serpent and every word from his mouth was like an ingredient in a recipe for death.

Lucy wanted to pull Garza away from Martin. She wanted to push Martin out of the door and tell him to run as fast as he could—far, far away. But she was petrified, and though her mind yearned for her to act, her body did nothing.

Garza embraced Martin and held him for a moment. "You're nothing like your father. You're nothing like us. But I've got this code, see, and I can't let you walk out of here."

Garza released Martin.

A mixture of fear and horror was all that was left in Martin's once warm countenance. He turned from Garza and began walking toward the door. He looked back toward Lucy, but she couldn't bear to watch.

Garza let the boy take a few more steps, then he raised his pistol and squeezed a single shot into the back of Martin's skull. Martin dropped to the floor, instantly.

Lucy screamed.

She lunged for the weapon, causing Garza to stumble. He recovered and aimed the gun at Lucy. Lucy considered the peace that would come if he pulled the trigger.

"Do it already," she said.

In that moment, Lucy understood that justice was a luxury. She was foolish to trust a man like Garza and thinking that killing Victor Soto would ever bring her peace. Lucy had only accomplished one thing—she helped Garza see that he wasn't washed up. He was the dog that had survived the backyard brawls, a bit chewed up and run down, but still with a deep, resonating hunger.

Lucy clung to Martin: "I'm sorry. I'm sorry," she said. Martin's thick blood pooled around them.

Garza lowered the pistol. "Leave him," Garza said, "there's nothing that can be done. Let's go."

The police sirens were getting closer—maybe a block or two away. Soon SWAT would arrive to kick down the door.

Lucy gripped Martin's body tighter.

"Go," she said, "get the fuck out! Leave us alone."

"Do you know what you're doing? If you're lucky they will arrest you."

"It doesn't matter anymore."

"And our agreement?" Garza asked.

"I won't say a word about you."

Garza positioned the pistol's handle in front of Lucy. "Take it," he said.

Lucy hesitated.

"This is the only way I can be sure you won't rat. Put your hand on the pistol."

Lucy knew she was signing her own life sentence. She also knew Garza would kill her if she didn't take the pistol, but she didn't know which the better choice was.

She opened her palm and Garza forced her hand around the pistol's grip.

Garza studied Lucy. "You're making a mistake staying here."

"I'll add it to all the other mistakes."

"You should be thanking me," Garza said, "I gave you what you wanted."

"Victor Soto is still alive."

"Maybe his heart beats but he's not alive. That boy down there was everything to him and he's been taken away. When he sees his body laid out on a slab, it'll be the end of Victor Soto. He'll wish he had died in that warehouse today—he'll wish his son had never been born, just so he wouldn't have to feel the pain. There are worse things than death, Lucy."

Lucy mumbled: "Martin."

"What?"

"His name was Martin—and he was my brother."

Garza gave an understanding nod. He opened the door and looked out before leaving Lucy in the apartment surrounded by death.

• • •

Ten minutes later, SWAT arrived and after Lucy ignored their orders to open the door, they rammed through with assault rifles. She put her hands up and an officer pushed her to the floor. She felt the throb of pain from her wound but said nothing. After she was cuffed, they pulled her up and walked her out of the apartment.

Outside, tenants who had been evacuated by LAPD stood with reporters and TV cameras. Lucy's face would be the one plastered all over the news—the worst kind of famous. She wondered what the newspapers would call her— "Little Girl Lost" or the "Punk Rock Killer"? She envisioned the trial; she'd be assigned a public defender but would fire him and secure a mid-ranged attorney with a ground floor office on the border of Beverly Hills—the east end of Wilshire Boulevard. Her lawyer would work *pro bono* because the case's publicity would be priceless. The prosecutor assigned would be a working pal of Victor Soto. And the personal connection to the family would make him a zealot in the pursuit of justice. There would be interviews with experts and TV personalities. In time, she'd be the subject of articles and books. And everyone would get justice except for Lucy. No matter how much she'd talk about her mother and what Victor Soto did, it wouldn't matter. Lucy's mother didn't matter in life, and she damn sure wouldn't matter in death. Garza would be proven right, mothers die every day and Lucy's mother was no different. Justice is something that must be bought with either money or influence. For Lucy, the only thing she was guilty of was attempting to tip the scale in her favor.

Lucy was put into an armored vehicle and shuttled to LAPD's Headquarters, the Central Community Station. During the interview, Lucy refused to answer even the most nonthreatening line of questioning. It was easy for her to fall mute again. She returned to that dark, quiet place that had existed in her mind; the same place she retreated to as a little girl upon learning of her mother's death.

During the interview, she requested a lawyer by writing it on a piece of paper and sliding it over to the lead detective. She didn't accept water or snacks, and though the chair she sat in had one leg that was shorter than the others, she didn't let it bother her. She knew it was something police did to keep suspects off balance and uncomfortable. But strangely, Lucy found comfort in knowing her fate.

Two female officers removed and bagged Lucy's clothes. She was given a blue shirt and matching pants like hospital scrubs, along with slip-on shoes to wear and was placed, alone, in a holding cell. She laid on the firm mattress, closed her eyes but couldn't sleep; she could only think of Martin and what she had become—a monster, an abomination— and she realized there were far worse things than prison and death. Lucy lacked the constitution for suicide; her only option was to live. But it would not be a life, Lucy thought, but rather a torment filled existence and she accepted this reality.

CHAPTER FOURTEEN

GARZA HAD SUCCESSFULLY hitch-hiked his way east towards the Inland Empire. There, an immigrant family picked him up on their way to Nevada. He had them drop him off in Riverside, where he loitered in front of a home improvement store with other brown-skinned men. The men were looking for work, construction, demolition, or otherwise. He watched as men hopped into truck beds to be driven out to worksites. When night fell, and the store began closing, he waited until all the customers' cars had left the parking lot. Soon, the overnight crew arrived, and he watched for the worker whose car would be the easiest to steal—something late modeled without an alarm. Garza settled on an old Ford Taurus with missing hubcaps. He didn't bother breaking the window; the worker had left the driver's side window partially down. Garza reached in and unlocked the car from the inside. It didn't take long for him to hotwire it.

He drove out of the parking lot and towards the highway. There was a small town that was best for laying low, north of Palm Springs. It was the type of place no one would bother him, if he kept to himself. He'd stay for a few weeks and watch the news for any mention of his name or the search for an accomplice in Lucy's case. If the focus was on Lucy, he'd have less to worry about. Victor Soto had seen him but knew nothing more than that Garza was an old man who drove a van. Southern California was full of men who matched his description. Without Lucy's cooperation, Soto and the police wouldn't have a solid lead. Garza would remain a ghost.

He drove through the blackness of the desert, never exceeding 50 mph, though the speed limit was 70, he wanted to drive unnoticed—and the car rumbled at 55. At times, he thought of his dead wife, Maria, and the son he had lost, and Gazpacho, the dog he had rescued. Garza knew he wasn't a good man and that all the loss he suffered he truly deserved, but he refused to accept it lying down. He was reminded of an old saying, a philosophy he thought he had abandoned— if life was brutal, then he would be brutal, too. It was cause and effect, and with each blow life delivered, Garza would inflict that type of pain ten times over on the most deserving—he'd balance the equation, equal the playing field. And God help whoever got in his way.

Garza tuned the radio to an AM sports channel broadcasting the last inning of the Dodger game. The Dodgers were up by three and their best hitter was about to bat. There was something about baseball that made everything okay. He turned up the volume and rolled the window down lower. The cool air whistled as the car pushed into the night.

ACKNOWLEDGMENTS

A special thanks to Gary Phillips.

AARON PHILIP CLARK is a novelist and screenwriter from Los Angeles, CA. His work has been praised by James Sallis, Gar Anthony Haywood, Gary Phillips, Eric Beetner, and Roger Smith. In addition to his writing career, he has worked in the film industry and law enforcement. Clark currently teaches English and writing courses at a university in Southern California.

To learn more about him, please visit AaronPhilipClark. com.

BOOKS

On the following pages are a few
more great titles from the
Down & Out Books publishing family.

For a complete list of books and to
sign up for our newsletter,
go to **DownAndOutBooks.com**.

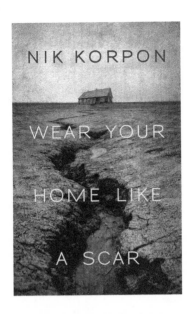

Wear Your Home Like A Scar
Nik Korpon

Down & Out Books
May 2019
978-1-948235-82-2

A clandestine surgeon goes to extreme lengths when she's torn between family loyalties. A con man tries to help his girlfriend escape her pimp, despite what the tarot cards tell her. A drifter hunts down the man who hung her out to dry with a cartel boss. A sicario has a crisis of faith when an old legend stalks him.

From the streets of Baltimore to the comunas of Medellín, the Mexican Sierras to Texas border towns, *Wear Your Home Like a Scar* shows that no matter how deep you cut, you'll never truly leave your home behind.

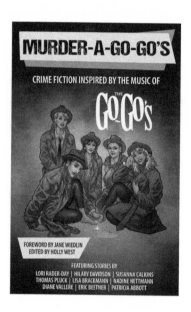

Murder-A-Go-Go's
Crime Fiction Inspired by the Music of The Go-Go's
Edited by Holly West

Down & Out Books
March 2019
978-1-948235-62-4

The Go-Go's made music on their own terms and gave voice to a generation caught between the bra-burning irreverence of the seventies and the me-first decadence of the eighties.

With a foreword by Go-Go's co-founder Jane Wiedlin and original stories by twenty-five kick-ass authors, editor Holly West has put together an all-star crime fiction anthology.

Main Bad Guy
A Love & Bullets Hookup
Nick Kolakowski

Shotgun Honey, an imprint of
Down & Out Books
978-1-948235-70-9

Bill and Fiona, the lovable anti-heroes of the "Love & Bullets" trilogy, find themselves in the toughest of tough spots: badly wounded, hunted by cops and goons, and desperately in need of a drink (or five).

After a round-the-world tour of spectacular criminality, they're back in New York. Locked in a panic room on the top floor of a skyscraper, surrounded by pretty much everyone in three zip codes who wants to kill them, they'll need to figure out how to stay upright and breathing… and maybe deal out a little payback in the process.

Gravy Train
Tess Makovesky

All Due Respect, an imprint of
Down & Out Books
978-1-64396-006-7

When barmaid Sandra wins eighty grand on a betting scam she thinks she's got it made. But she's reckoned without an assortment of losers and criminals, including a mugger, a car thief and even her own step-uncle George.

As they hurtle towards a frantic showdown by the local canal, will Sandra see her ill-gotten gains again? Or will her precious gravy train come shuddering to a halt?